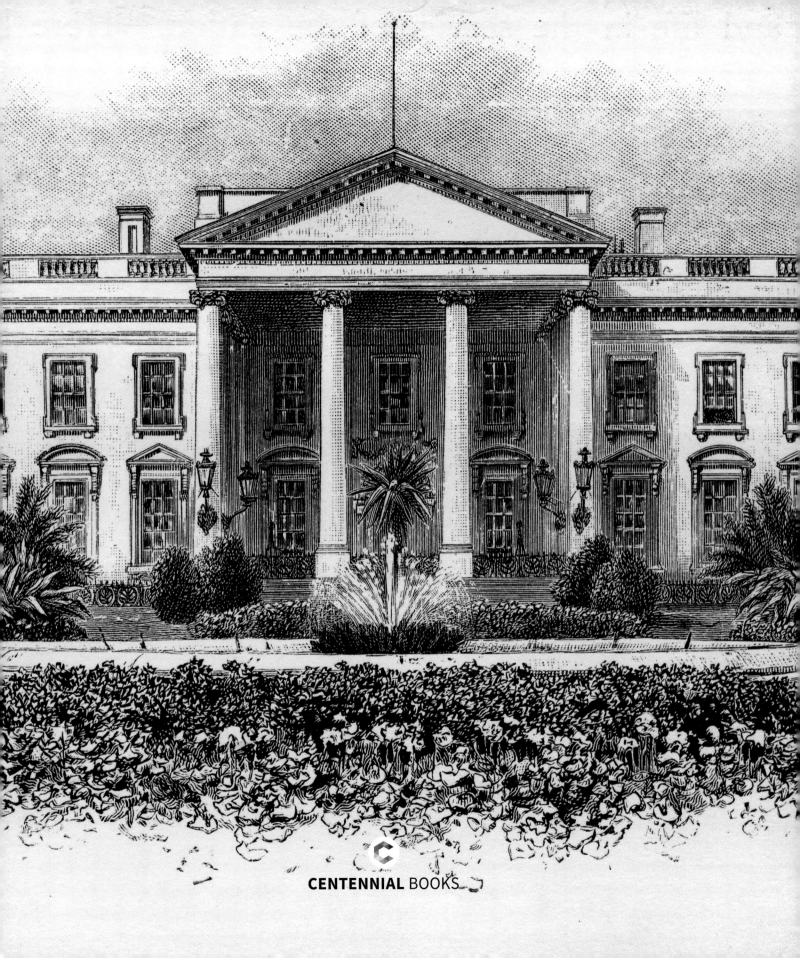

The
WHITE HOUSE
ATLAS

A COMPLETE ILLUSTRATED GUIDE TO
1600 PENNSYLVANIA AVENUE

★

BY NICOLE WETSMAN

CONTENTS

30 | 92

160 | 16

5

WELCOME TO THE

WHITE HOUSE

CHAPTER 1

PLANNING *the* PRESIDENT'S PALACE

★ ★ ★

"I PRAY HEAVEN TO BESTOW THE BEST OF BLESSINGS ON THIS HOUSE, AND ON ALL THAT SHALL HEREAFTER INHABIT IT. MAY NONE BUT HONEST AND WISE MEN EVER RULE UNDER THIS ROOF."

PRESIDENT JOHN ADAMS

THE PRESIDENTIAL HOME'S first architect, Pierre Charles L'Enfant, had a grand vision for the capital city as well as the president's house. L'Enfant's preliminary city drawings *(opposite)* reveal plans for a house of a grand scale in the style of French palaces. The grounds would be surrounded by a magnificent setting with a pond and water features in the tradition of French Baroque gardens.

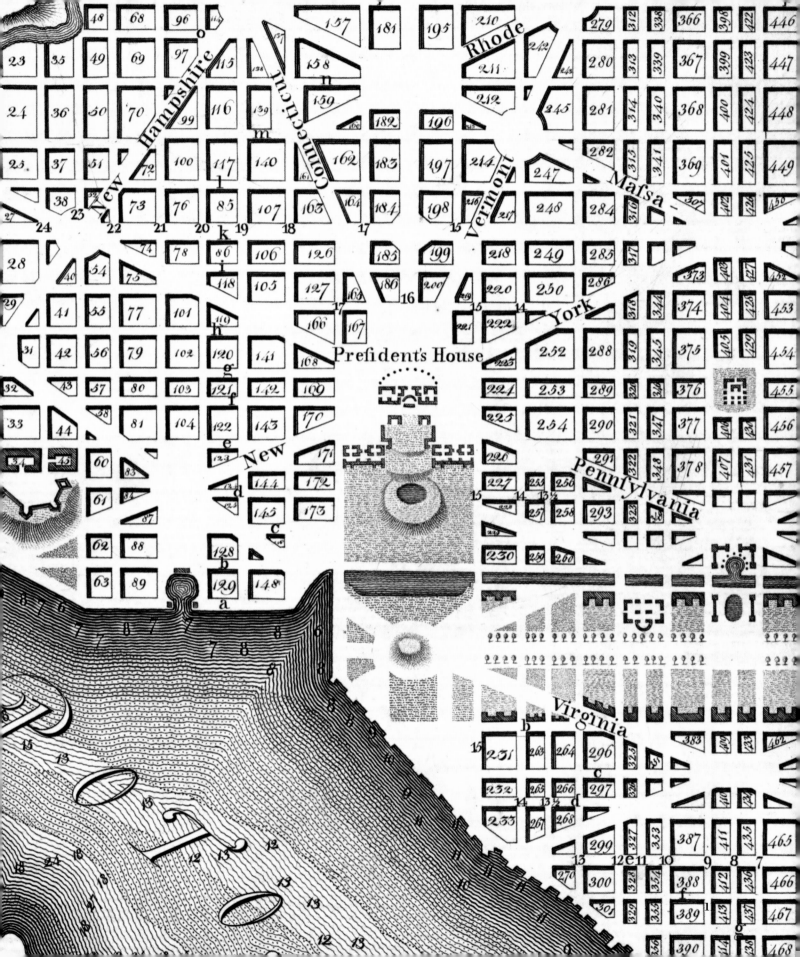

IN 1791, GEORGE WASHINGTON, the young nation's first president, set out to build a capital city on the shores of the Potomac River from land that had been ceded by Maryland and Virginia. The ambitious project was led by French engineer and architect Pierre Charles L'Enfant, who envisioned in the lush landscape a shimmering city that would become the center of the government. For L'Enfant, one of the most significant aspects of this endeavor would be what he called the "President's Palace." "His federal city was to be the grand embodiment of a great nation yet to be," writes historian William Seale in his book The President's House. *"Major L'Enfant imagined the house for the President as a crucial feature of his city plan."*

L'Enfant would not see his vision come to fruition, however. By February 1792 he had fallen out of favor with the commissioners leading the city planning, and Washington as well, and was fired for insubordination. In March of that year, the commissioners held a competition to complete the project. Advertised in local newspapers, the contest offered a $500 cash prize and a medal for the best design of a president's house. James Hoban, an Irish-born architect, produced the winning plan, which was modeled after the Leinster House, the seat of the parliament in Ireland. He took home the medal.

Washington admired Hoban's neoclassical country house design that was a familiar style in England and Ireland. His main quibble was the scale. Washington ordered the house to be enlarged by one-fifth and dressed up with carvings and ornamentation.

Construction on the building began in October of 1792. The structure was built from Aquia Creek sandstone, pulled from Virginia's Stafford County. Washington selected the stone for the president's

AN ENGRAVING OF THE damaged White House "after the conflagration" in 1814 *(opposite)*. During the War of 1812, the United States was at war against Great Britain, and British soldiers invaded Washington, D.C., torching government buildings. In addition to the president's house, the U.S. Capitol, the Treasury and the War Department were in ruins. James Hoban was asked to rebuild the presidential home. The east and west ends of the building had been completely destroyed by the fire. President James Madison, who was president when the British attacked, would not return to the home. President James Monroe moved into the restored house in 1817.

house—something he had done for other government buildings as well. In total, the project cost $232,372 and took eight years to complete. It was, at the time, the largest house in the country and would retain that distinction until after the Civil War.

Though he handpicked the architect and oversaw the construction, Washington never actually lived in the house. With other structures in the city, including the Capitol, being built concurrently, the presidential manor was unfinished when Washington's presidency came to an end in 1797.

It wouldn't be inhabited until 1800, when John Adams and his wife, Abigail, moved in. Even though the building was still under construction, Abigail recognized the home as a "castle."

After it was completed, the house was periodically painted over with whitewash, primarily to protect the sandstone from freezing. In 1818, the walls were colored white with a more permanent, lead-based paint. By that point, it had been known as the "White House" for about a decade. The widely used nickname was unofficial until 1901, when Theodore Roosevelt formalized the moniker.

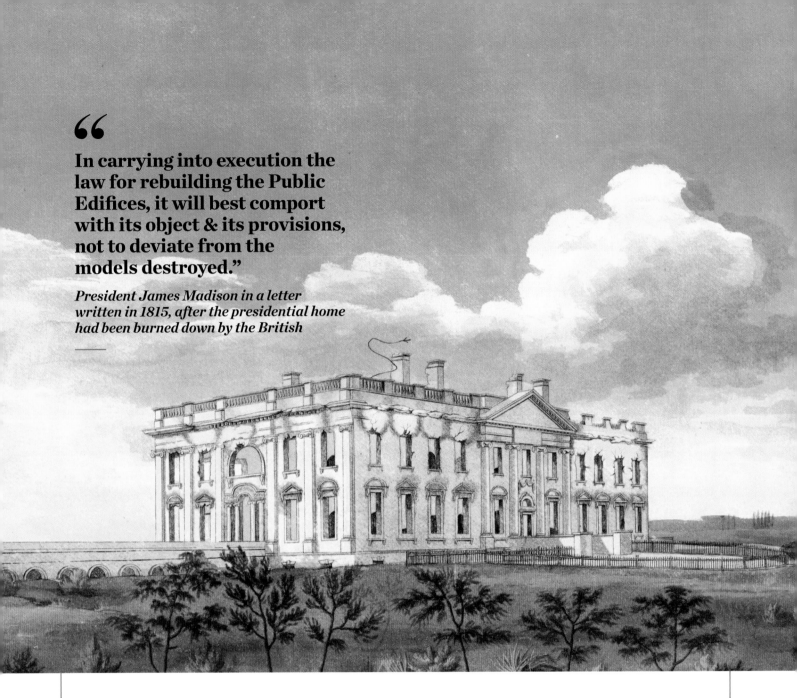

In the 200 years since it was built, the White House has seen enormous change: It was destroyed by a fire, has gone through numerous renovations, and received modern additions and new rooms. Dignitaries, politicians and celebrities pay visits, and each day, hundreds of people line up by the gates to snap photos. Throughout all of our many shifts and changes, the White House has been the centerpiece of United States history.

While it was initially envisioned as a palace for the president, over the years it's become clear that the White House is a symbol of our country's democratic ideals. As a *Washington Post* editorial once noted, "The White House is not the president's property. Indeed, the president's lease may be a very short one."

A MAP TO THE BUILDING

Few structures around the world—if any—serve as many crucial functions as the White House. It's the command center of the U.S., where each decision made by the president ripples outward to affect the world at large. It's where international dignitaries convene with the American government for diplomatic meetings and state dinners. It's the site of events for the public, like the annual White House Easter Egg Roll. And last but not least, it's a home. The president can never fully escape the pressures of the position, but quality time with his family in the White House residence is as close as he'll get.

1. THE OVAL OFFICE
Established in its current location by President Franklin D. Roosevelt in 1933, the Oval Office is the president's primary workspace and where he hosts the majority of his meetings.

2. THE CABINET ROOM
The vice president, secretary of state and more join the president around an oval mahogany table to discuss the issues of the day. The Cabinet Room overlooks the Rose Garden.

3. BLUE ROOM
Named for its all-blue decor, the Blue Room acts as a reception room for guests of the president. With a stunning view of the South Lawn, it makes for quite the first impression.

4. EAST ROOM
The largest room in the building, the East Room hosts major White House events. It is also often the site of private inaugurations for incoming presidents.

5. OFFICE OF THE FIRST LADY
The Office of the First Lady has moved locations several times and has evolved alongside the expectations of the role. Eleanor Roosevelt had two staffers; Hillary Clinton had 20.

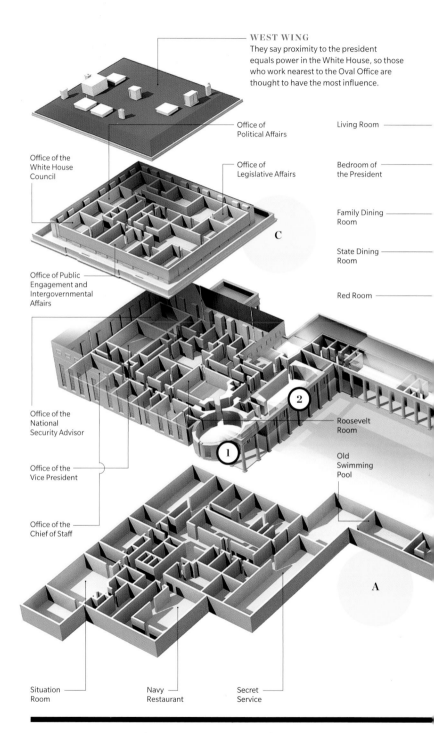

WEST WING
They say proximity to the president equals power in the White House, so those who work nearest to the Oval Office are thought to have the most influence.

Office of the White House Council

Office of Public Engagement and Intergovernmental Affairs

Office of the National Security Advisor

Office of the Vice President

Office of the Chief of Staff

Office of Political Affairs

Office of Legislative Affairs

Living Room

Bedroom of the President

Family Dining Room

State Dining Room

Red Room

Roosevelt Room

Old Swimming Pool

C

2

1

A

Situation Room

Navy Restaurant

Secret Service

A. BASEMENT
Sub-basement added during the Truman Administration.

B. GROUND FLOOR
Throughout the 1800s, it was known as the "basement."

C. FIRST FLOOR
Called the "State Floor" for its formal receptions.

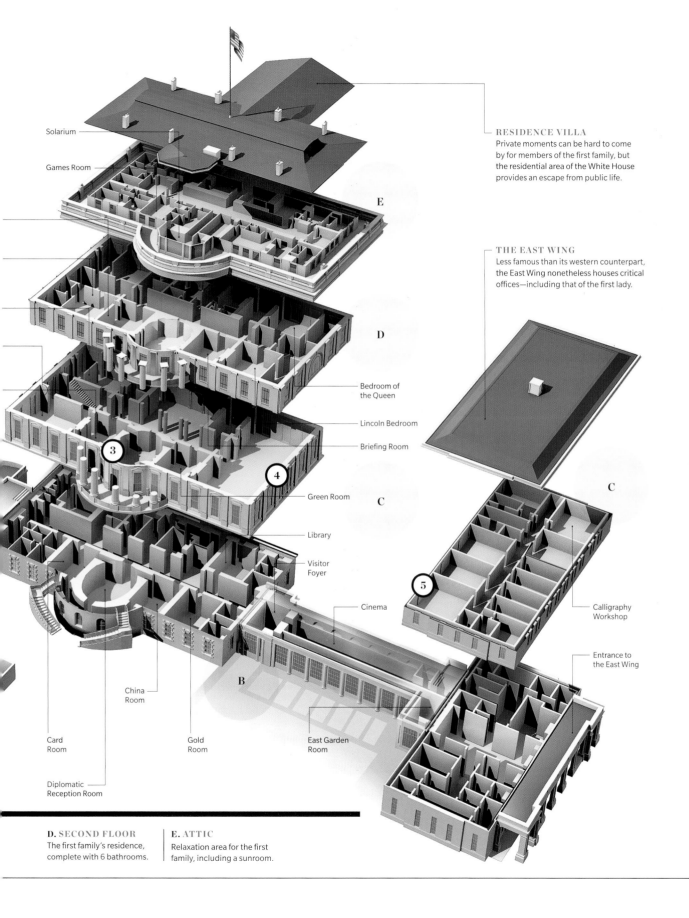

Solarium

Games Room

E

RESIDENCE VILLA
Private moments can be hard to come
by for members of the first family, but
the residential area of the White House
provides an escape from public life.

THE EAST WING
Less famous than its western counterpart,
the East Wing nonetheless houses critical
offices—including that of the first lady.

D

Bedroom of
the Queen

Lincoln Bedroom

Briefing Room

C

C

3

4

Green Room

Library

5

Visitor
Foyer

Calligraphy
Workshop

Cinema

Entrance to
the East Wing

B

China
Room

Card
Room

Gold
Room

East Garden
Room

Diplomatic
Reception Room

D. SECOND FLOOR
The first family's residence,
complete with 6 bathrooms.

E. ATTIC
Relaxation area for the first
family, including a sunroom.

★

CHAPTER 2

The WEST WING

★ ★ ★

THE HEART OF THE EXECUTIVE BRANCH – AND THE CENTER OF THE ACTION AND POWER – LIE IN THIS FAMOUS BUILDING.

THE BUILDING NOW known as the West Wing was built by Theodore Roosevelt in 1902, beyond the west terrace of the White House grounds. At the time, it housed the offices of his secretary and staff, but the president continued to officially preside from the main residence. In 1933, Franklin D. Roosevelt expanded the West Wing to the structure we are familiar with today. He moved and rebuilt the Oval Office to the east, where it overlooks the Rose Garden.

"**THE WEST WING** *of the White House may be the most formidable power stage in the world," wrote Hugh Sidey, a journalist who covered the presidency for nearly five decades. Indeed, in modern U.S. history, no place has been the center of more historically significant events than the West Wing. Since it was built in 1902, this area of the White House grounds has been the place where the executive branch carries out its critical duties.* ⟶

THE OVAL Office was built under the watch of President William Howard Taft; here, on January 6, 1912, he signed the act admitting New Mexico to the Union.

FRANKLIN D. ROOSEVELT working in the West Wing; here, he would guide the country through difficult times and sign important bills that changed the nation, such as the Social Security Act of 1935.

I t has witnessed transformative bills signed into law, the country enter into world wars (and come to the brink of nuclear war), a presidential resignation, and the most wanted terrorist alive hunted down. On a day-to-day basis it remains the nerve center of the executive branch, abuzz with hundreds of staffers and advisers, members of the press covering the White House and the president running the country from his desk in the Oval Office.

In the early years of the presidential home, the mansion did not have official work areas. But in the 19th century, as the president's staff and cabinet grew, office space became concentrated on the second floor of the main residence. Following the assassination of Abraham Lincoln, the new president, Andrew Johnson, tried to bring order to a chaotic time by expanding offices in the White House. In addition to his office, he created a reception room, an office for his secretary, a common office with six desks, a Cabinet room and the first telegraph room.

But even as more official space was allotted, the staff quickly outgrew the rooms. In 1902, President Theodore Roosevelt moved the offices to a separate building on the west grounds of the White House. The newly minted Executive Office Building would come to be known as the West Wing. Roosevelt's West Wing was smaller than today's, and the president worked in a rectangular room—now, it's a meeting room called the Roosevelt Room. Seven years later, President William Howard Taft doubled the size of the building and constructed the first Oval Office. Congress had appropriated $40,000 for the additional accommodations, and he selected a local architect named Nathan Wyeth to do the work. "I have endeavored to show a dignified treatment in keeping with the high purpose it is to serve," Wyeth said ⟶

66

I have a nice home, the office is close by, and the pay is good."

President John F. Kennedy

——

ON JUNE 10, 1963, John F. Kennedy signed the Equal Pay Act, one of the first laws aimed at guaranteeing pay parity for women. He acknowledged it as a first step: "Much remains to be done to achieve full equality of economic opportunity."

of his design. As William Seale notes in his book *The President's House*, "The plan changed the symbolic character of the Executive Office Building from a staff office into an office for the President."

Taft's Oval Office featured an olive green color scheme; each president in turn puts his own decorative touch on the space. Before John F. Kennedy's death, his wife, Jacqueline, had planned to redecorate the Oval Office with a deep-red carpet and pale drapes. Richard Nixon preferred a navy blue rug with

ON AUGUST 28, 1974, President Gerald Ford held his first press conference after assuming office in the East Room of the White House.

gold drapes. When Donald Trump took office, he replaced Barack Obama's yellow wallpaper with a gray damask print and gold-hued upholstery.

Today, the modern West Wing is the central hub of activity for dozens of government officials. It holds various offices, a cafeteria and, on the ground floor, the Situation Room—a highly secured and soundproof conference room where officials and the president receive key intelligence and security information.

The most senior staff in the West Wing work from the first floor, close to the Oval Office. Senior advisers to the president, who help create policy on a wide range of areas, work from the two offices directly adjacent to the Oval. Other assorted advisers—deputy chief of staff, the director of the national economic council, speechwriters, various counselors to the president—also work in the halls of the West Wing, often in offices big enough to hold only a desk and a chair. In addition, the vice president has an office in the West Wing, as well as a set of offices in the Eisenhower Executive Office Building, located next to the White House.

The dozens of reporters who cover the daily activities of the president and the White House have been headquartered in the West Wing since 1970, when the White House Press Briefing Room was constructed. Nixon converted the room that previously housed an indoor pool that Franklin D. Roosevelt used daily. The press room has become a hot spot, especially during the →

THE U.S. AS A WORLD power is on full display in the West Wing. The area has been the site of diplomatic efforts, as foreign dignitaries are welcomed there during official visits. In 2005, President George W. Bush came together with British Prime Minister Tony Blair for a press conference to discuss famine-relief efforts in Africa.

Trump administration, as coverage has intensified on the White House and the number of media outlets continues to grow.

As the country has evolved and the administrations change, the West Wing has undergone renovations and expansions. But what remains the same is the importance of this hub. "The White House has been operating so long, in

JOE BIDEN, WHO served as vice president under Barack Obama, is shown working with his staff in 2009. The vice president's office in the West Wing is directly next to the office of the president's chief of staff.

so many times of crisis and challenge, that the working side of the West Wing conveys an atmosphere of calm and unhurried deliberation," wrote journalist Haynes Johnson in his 1975 book, *The Working White House.* "At the same time one cannot help but be struck by the remarkable efficiency and volume of work accomplished here. It seems effortless. Of course it is not."

THE FIRST LADIES OF THE WHITE HOUSE

ON THE OTHER side of the building, in the East Wing, the first lady has a suite of offices where her staffers and advisers assist in creating policy around her work. The president may be the one voted into office, but over the years, the role of the first lady has proven to be one of incredible influence and power. In addition to overseeing the running of the White House, first ladies champion important causes. Eleanor Roosevelt, wife of Franklin D. Roosevelt, was as savvy a politician as her husband. The activist later served as the first chair of the U.N. Commission on Human Rights. The more recent first ladies' platforms have included literacy, children's health, helping military families and cyberbullying. Their work leaves a lasting impact on everyday Americans. As Barack Obama said of his wife, Michelle, "You made the White House a place that belongs to everybody. And a new generation sets its sights higher because it has you as a role model."

IT'S CUSTOMARY FOR THE outgoing first lady to give her successor a personal tour of her soon-to-be home. Here, Laura Bush showed Michelle Obama the Green Room in the East Wing on the morning of Barack Obama's inauguration in 2009.

★

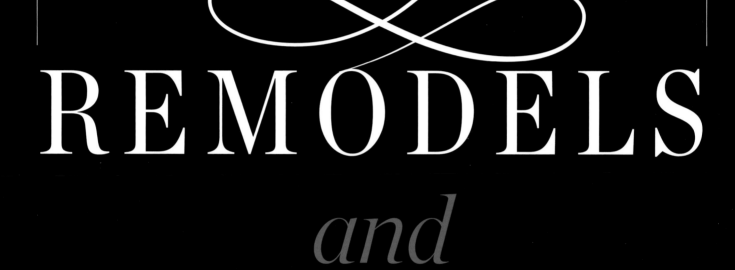

CHAPTER 3

REMODELS

and

RENOVATIONS

⋙⟶

★ ★ ★

THE ICONIC MANSION HAS UNDERGONE MANY MAKEOVERS THROUGH THE YEARS, THOUGH NONE BIGGER THAN IN 1949.

SOON AFTER THE Truman family came to the White House in 1945, President Harry Truman noticed floor-to-ceiling cracks and heard the house creak and groan. His daughter Margaret's piano broke through the floorboards and knocked down plaster off the dining room ceiling below. Determined to address any danger in the structure, Truman appointed a commission to do an in-depth analysis. The following year, the great Truman renovation of the White House was underway. The opposite image is a view of the northeast corner of the White House during work in 1950. Truman made sure to keep the outside of the structure unchanged during the massive project.

WHEN PRESIDENT HARRY TRUMAN *moved into the White House in 1945, almost a century and a half after John Adams had become its first resident, the home was firmly established as a magnificent symbol from the outside. But inside, it was crumbling. According to White House historian William Seale, Truman liked to call the White House a place where "some lived it up and others wore it down."* ⟶

IN 1949, officials looked over the bold plans for the White House (*above*). Congress had approved an appropriation of $5.4 million for the work.

AFTER THE STRUCTURE was gutted to its stone walls, temporary steel bracing provided support in 1950. The concrete underpinnings for the walls allowed large construction vehicles to dig a new basement.

Indeed, after all the years of expansions and wear and tear, the structure was in dire need of an overhaul. A Secret Service report during World War II had already found the White House to be a dangerous fire trap. Truman asked for further inspections when he moved in. "The engineer said that the ceiling in the state dining room only stayed up from force of habit," Truman wrote to his sister in 1948. The walls were cracked; the floors sagged. A stress test of the second-floor oval room was found to be unsafe if more than 15 people occupied it. Change was needed. Truman would go on to see the most ambitious renovation of the presidential home since a fire burned down much of the White House in 1814 (see p. 43).

The Truman renovation was certainly not the first time the White House had undergone a makeover. In fact, Thomas Jefferson hardly let the paint dry on the initial construction before putting his mark on the mansion. When he succeeded Adams as president in 1801, he started on the first renovation. Jefferson constructed an ice house to keep food and drink cold, upgraded the kitchen and installed water closets. He also hired architect Benjamin Latrobe as the

> "
> **[The White House] tries to be a spacious and dignified dwelling and nothing more, and in this it is entirely successful."**
>
> *Journalist E. V. Smalley, in 1884, on the evolution of the building*

THESE ENGRAVINGS (*above*) illustrate the White House's North Portico (*left*) and South Portico (*right*) in the 1800s. Both were extensions of the original house.

surveyor of public buildings and worked with him to begin the additions of two domestic-service wings to the existing building. Jefferson turned the entrance hall of the White House into a museum filled with artifacts from the West—including some collected by Meriwether Lewis and William Clark—and opened the mansion and the grounds to the public.

Over the years, the outside saw a number of additions: The South Portico of the building was created in 1824, followed five years later by the North Portico, which serves as the entranceway to the White House. President John Quincy Adams created the first White House flower garden in 1825 and added trees to those planted by Jefferson during his term in office.

In 1881, Chester Arthur turned his attention to the interior. He spent $110,000—the most since the home's reconstruction in 1814—on refurbishing the White House, hiring Louis Comfort Tiffany, the first design director of the famous Tiffany & Co, to lead the project. "It can be supposed that Arthur, the sophisticated New Yorker, was repelled by the 'department-store' or 'upholstery-shop' look of the White House," wrote Seale in *The President's House*. "He ⟶

> ## When the job is finished, everyone will like it."

President Truman, in 1948, on the controversial addition of a balcony on the White House's South Portico

―――

ordered a second redecoration of the state rooms, six months after the completion of the first…. The sort of interior the President had in mind required an artist's touch."

Tiffany was precisely that kind of designer. He focused on the play of natural light on objects, as well as mixing color schemes and patterns to elevate the aesthetic of the historic rooms. He also created an opulent, colorful glass screen, which stood in the entrance hall.

The early 20th century saw the major additions of the West Wing and Oval Office, but many improvements were hastily done, and the integrity of the structure grew more and more worrisome. Truman's renovations were not about beautification as much as necessity. Engineers went so far as to recommend that the entire White House be torn down and rebuilt, an idea that Truman rejected. He held great regard for the history of the mansion and what it meant to the country. Truman made sure to keep the external walls so that the outside didn't look different to the public. The inside, however, was uninhabitable. During the construction, which lasted from 1949 to 1952, Truman and his family lived across the street in the Blair House.

Before the renovation, the White House had 62 rooms, 26 halls and 14 bathrooms. When the Trumans moved back in on March 27, 1952, there were more than 100

MEN WORKING ON THE exterior walls of the White House (*opposite*) in August 1945.

TRUMAN'S FIRST MAJOR White House change was the addition of a second-floor balcony on the South Portico (*above*). Many opposed the balcony and how it impacted the look of the historic building, but it has become one of the most recognizable features of the White House exterior.

rooms, 40 halls and 19 bathrooms. Truman took the nation on a tour of the grand new home in a live national television special.

Today, Congress allocates money to allow incoming presidents to redecorate and update furnishings. The president and the first lady can change the living spaces to suit their own tastes, and often make selections from the collection of furniture that the White House keeps in storage. The look may change, but Truman's structural modernization remains as he had built it. Wrote Seale: "President Truman had done what he set out to do: rebuild the house for all time."

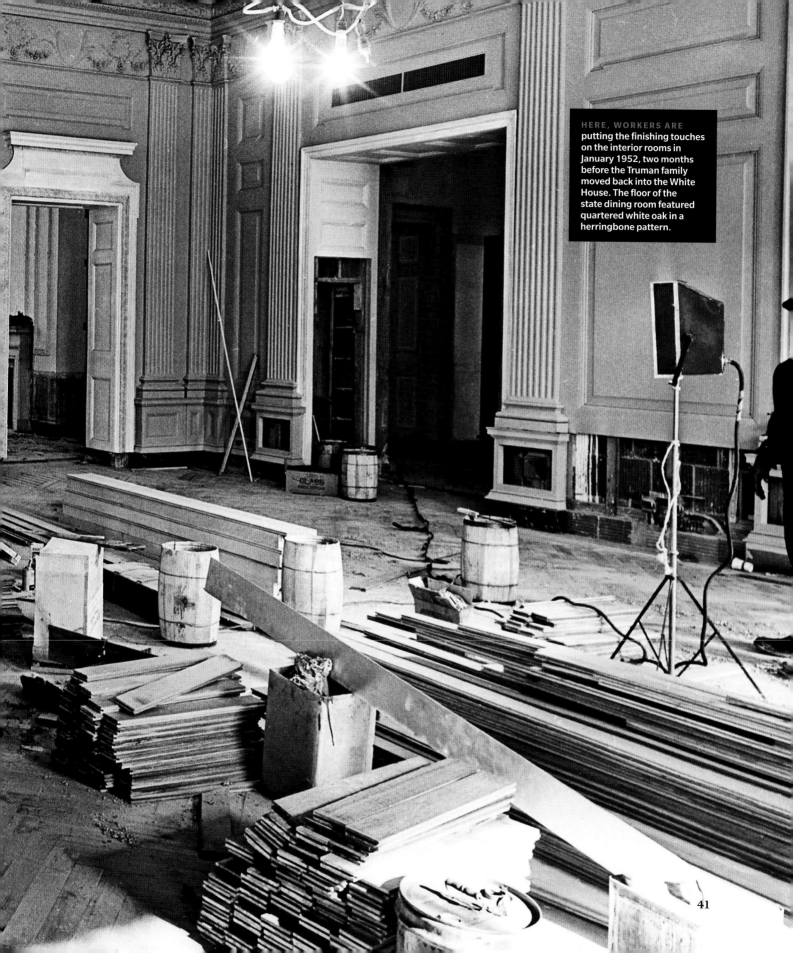

HERE, WORKERS ARE putting the finishing touches on the interior rooms in January 1952, two months before the Truman family moved back into the White House. The floor of the state dining room featured quartered white oak in a herringbone pattern.

FIRST LADY JACQUELINE
Kennedy looked over plans in July 1961 during the White House restoration she oversaw, while White House curator Lorraine Pearce spoke on the phone. Jackie saw to it that the White House was designated a museum to help preserve it, and also created the White House Historical Association to publicize its heritage.

THE GREAT FIRE

THE WHITE HOUSE underwent its first major overhaul after the War of 1812. Less than 30 years after the end of the Revolutionary War, British soldiers had invaded American soil again, and in August 1814, they stormed Washington, D.C., and set fire to the federal buildings. Before fleeing the attack, first lady Dolley Madison famously saved a portrait of George Washington hanging in the White House (although experts now say that was actually a copy). When British soldiers got to the White House, they found the table set for a dinner party. They ate the prepared food—and then burned the place down.

Congress contemplated moving the capital out of Washington but decided to stay put and rebuild the destroyed structures. James Hoban, the original architect, was brought on to put the burned shell of the president's house back together. The stone walls remained largely intact, and it took Hoban only three years to reconstruct what had originally taken him 10—though in order to speed things along, he used timber, rather than the original brick, a decision that would contribute to later structural problems. Even today, there are still visible scorch marks on the White House stone.

PRESIDENT LYNDON JOHNSON'S THREE televisions kept him apprised of the news while he sat at a mahogany pedestal partners desk (built by the Senate Cabinet Shop in the early 1900s). He opted for FDR's blue-green rug and JFK's pale curtains, and displayed portraits of Andrew Jackson, Thomas Jefferson and FDR.

PRESIDENT BILL CLINTON'S daughter, Chelsea, played with Socks the cat in the Oval Office, which was updated to feature a navy blue rug and gold damask drapes with a pattern once used by George Washington. Clinton worked from the 1880 Resolute desk used by Kennedy (and kept by George W. Bush), carved from the timbers of the British ship *H.M.S. Resolute* and given to Rutherford B. Hayes as a gift by Queen Victoria. The red-and-white striped sofas added to the patriotic decor.

PRESIDENT BARACK OBAMA'S OVAL
Office featured deep-red curtains and striped wallpaper. His cream-colored rug had the presidential seal in the center, and quotations from Abraham Lincoln, John F. Kennedy, Theodore Roosevelt, Franklin D. Roosevelt and Martin Luther King Jr. around the edge.

PRESIDENT DONALD TRUMP
spent $3.4 million to refurbish the White House in 2017. He changed the furnishings of the Oval Office and used plenty of gold throughout. His red-and-beige carpet with green leaves was used briefly by President George W. Bush, and originated in the Ronald Reagan era.

★

CHAPTER 4

The
PRIVATE
RESIDENCE

★ ★ ★

WHEN THE PRESIDENT LEAVES THE OFFICE TO GO HOME AT THE END OF THE DAY, ALL HE HAS TO DO IS WALK UPSTAIRS.

WHEN IT COMES down to it, the first family is just like any other when the workday ends—eating together, perhaps entertaining friends or watching TV, and putting their children to bed. Here, first lady Jacqueline Kennedy spent time reading a bedtime story to her children, Caroline (in a medieval princess costume) and John Jr., in August 1962.

AFTER THE BUSINESS of the day had wrapped up and the staff of the West Wing was out the door, President Barack Obama would make his way back to the White House residence, a few steps away. He'd sit down to dinner—a meal prepared by a world-class chef—with his family. Then he would maybe shoot some pool in the game room before tucking his daughters into bed and heading off to his home office, the Treaty Room, on the second floor of the residence. ⟶

THE LINCOLN sitting room, renovated by first lady Hillary Clinton in 1993, is next to the Lincoln Bedroom; it got its name when Harry Truman asked that it be fitted with Lincoln-era furnishings.

51

With sports on low, Obama would turn to his daily briefing and check in on his games of Words With Friends. The kitchen, with endless options, would only be a phone call away, but he famously snacked only on salted almonds. Between midnight and 2 a.m., he'd go down the hall to bed.

For the president, the workplace of the powerful executive branch of the United States Government doubles as the family home. The White House may be a grand, historic building, more museum than house, but presidents have worked to make the second and third floors, which are private spaces for the first family, feel like home.

New presidents put their own personal stamp on the residence. "It says something about their style," Washington historian Carl Anthony told *The New York Times.* "It can be a symbol, a political statement. It reflects the way the president and his family see themselves in the world."

The first family gets a budget of $100,000 to spend on redecorating, although some presidents decline the money and pay out of pocket (or use funds donated for this purpose) for new wallpaper and couches.

Most presidents and first ladies take the second-floor suite as their bedroom—a large space with two bathrooms and a view over the Potomac River. Donald Trump and his wife, Melania, reportedly have separate bedrooms. Presidents have maintained different levels of privacy over their living quarters. First lady Laura Bush offered documentary crews a tour, while the Obamas cordoned off the residence area—only offering photographs before Obama left office.

Security in the private residence is nonnegotiable. Windows have to ⟶

"
I don't like a lot of frills and fusses."
First lady Nancy Reagan

NANCY REAGAN'S favorite color was red, and it shows in this second-floor study, where in 1981, she and husband Ronald ate their dinners off silver trays.

FIRST LADY BETTY FORD was dressed to match the decor in 1975 in the Yellow Oval Room, which is part of the first family's second-floor residence. In different administrations, the room has been used as a living room, a library and an office.

remain closed, and the members of the first family can't stray far from their bedrooms without a security detail.

The president and first family are served by a permanent staff of nearly 100 people in the residence, with more working part time. Butlers, maids, doormen, chefs and more fill out the roster, and the White House chief usher oversees them all. The staff is everywhere, and at the same time, invisible—keeping the household running smoothly for some very important people. "There was never a dull day," said Lillian Rogers Parks, who worked as a maid and seamstress at the White House for over 30 years. Open positions are generally passed down to friends and family, and most people who work as staffers in the White House remain there for decades. It's no wonder, then, that they often develop close relationships with the first family.

Staff are privy to intimate moments, like when an usher had an urgent message for President Ronald Reagan, who was in the shower. The staff is also trained to keep an eye out for any potential security risks. Most are career White House employees, staying in place even as the administration changes, so they know the building and its day-to-day functions intimately.

The president is fed by a talented chef and staff who can prepare anything the first family is craving. The food that arrives at the White House is carefully screened by the Secret Service to ensure its safety. The president can still order takeout—as long as it's ordered to another location, so the restaurant doesn't know who it's for. Through the years, White House chefs have been asked to prepare some strange foods. Former chef Roland Mesnier remembered being asked to prepare a Clinton family recipe: "An atrocious concoction of Coca-Cola–flavored jelly served with black glacé cherries."

Living in the White House comes with its perks, but the first family doesn't have

IN 1974, GERALD FORD —who became president after the resignation of Richard Nixon earlier that year—prepared his own English muffin in a small kitchen in the White House.

a free ride through their four (or eight) years spent living there. The president is sent a bill each month for food, dry cleaning, staff and other expenses. Just like any other household, grocery bills are the president's responsibility, not the taxpayers'.

LYNDON JOHNSON would sometimes hold staff meetings, like this one in 1966, in the spare bedroom.

FIRST DAUGHTER LUCI
Johnson blew out the candles as her dad held her birthday cake in 1964.

FIRST LADY ROSALYNN Carter dined with her children, grandchild and mother-in-law.

FIRST DAUGHTER Margaret Truman, a soprano singer, posed in the family's quarters in 1950 after giving a White House concert.

FIRST LADY BARBARA Bush bonded with Princess Diana during a 1990 visit.

PRESIDENT GEORGE W. Bush and the first family visited with the previous first family, including his parents, former President George H. W. Bush and Barbara.

FIRST DAUGHTER AMY Carter and her mom, Rosalynn, enjoyed a chef's tour of the White House kitchen.

PRESIDENT RICHARD NIXON
and his wife, Pat, had coffee on
the balcony, with a view of the
Washington Monument.

AIR FORCE ONE HAS
4,000 square feet of space
for the president and fellow
passengers to enjoy.

"THE BEAST" IS BASED
on a Cadillac and made
by GM. The current model
was built in 2018.

GROUND FORCE ONE is an armored bus that transports the president and other dignitaries.

NAVY ONE WAS BUILT by Lockheed, and can land on an aircraft carrier.

HOW THE PRESIDENT COMES AND GOES

THE PRESIDENT'S FIRST trip to his new home leads from the steps of the Capitol, where the oath of office is taken, and down Pennsylvania Avenue to the White House. Traditionally, the new president rides most of the way in a limousine but emerges to walk and wave to the crowds who line the streets.

Once in office, travel for the president becomes a logistical ballet. The limo, nicknamed "The Beast," is an armored vehicle with protections to prevent the fuel tank from exploding or the tires from puncturing. The back seat is equipped with Wi-Fi and a satellite phone, and night vision cameras and shotguns are easily accessible in the front seat. Route cars and police on motorcycles forge ahead of the president's vehicle, which follows closely behind a lead car. Support vehicles, often carrying staff, and various communications, protection and intelligence vehicles, follow behind. An ambulance and rear guard are at the end of the procession, and a helicopter follows overhead.

The president flies on Air Force One, which functions as an airborne command center—it holds a conference room, communications equipment and an onboard medical suite. It has three levels and can feed 100 people out of two galleys. The plane can refuel in midair, so it has an unlimited range. Whether in flight or on the runway, Air Force One is one of the most easily recognizable symbols of the presidency.

★

CHAPTER 5

HISTORIC
FURNISHINGS

⋙⟶

★   ★   ★

THE WHITE HOUSE IS A LIVING MUSEUM, FEATURING IMPORTANT PIECES THAT TELL THE STORY OF OUR NATION'S HISTORY.

THE RED ROOM is the boldest of the White House state rooms, showcasing the strong hue on its walls and furnishings. First lady Nancy Reagan, known for her love of the color, took her official portrait in the Red Room *(opposite)*. The 36-light French Empire chandelier was fashioned from carved and gilded wood. Notable portraits displayed in the Red Room include an 1842 portrait of Angelica Singleton Van Buren (President Martin Van Buren's daughter-in-law) by Henry Inman, displayed above the mantel, and Gilbert Stuart's 1804 portrait of Dolley Madison.

RHODE ISLAND PAINTER *Gilbert Stuart was a preeminent American portraitist, committing masterful images of generals, socialites and politicians alike to canvas in the late 1700s and early 1800s. Perhaps his most famous work, though, is a full-length painting of George Washington, known as the Lansdowne portrait (saved by Dolley Madison during the War of 1812). In the image, Washington stands addressing Congress as president, surrounded by symbols of his roles in the war, the writing of the Constitution, and the genesis of the country.* ⟶

THE FAMOUS Lansdowne portrait *(above)* depicts a 64-year-old Washington in his last year as president. The artist Gilbert Stuart painted three copies of it, one of which hangs in the East Room of the White House.

LADY BIRD JOHNSON was photographed for *Vogue* in the Blue Room in 1964. The room's style was influenced by France's Napoleonic era.

Stuart completed the portrait in 1796, and in 1800, it was purchased using funds from the U.S. Treasury and put on display as the first piece of art in the newly completed White House.

Since then, along with its role as the home of the president and the seat of the executive branch of the government, the White House has functioned as an ever-changing museum with a vast collection of furniture, china, art and other furnishings. These items are declared the permanent property of the house in a law passed by Congress in 1961.

During the Kennedy administration, these furnishings were recognized as a cherished part of this nation's history. When John F. Kennedy and his family moved into the White House in 1961, first lady Jacqueline Kennedy was disappointed to find so few historic pieces in a home of so much significance. So she formed a Fine Arts Committee, acquiring authentic pieces like the original chairs from President James Monroe's Oval Room.

Fine art was also donated, and the famed French interior designer Stéphane Boudin oversaw the entire project. The state rooms were thoughtfully appointed and furnished to represent historical periods. The Green Room was in the Federal style; the Blue Room, reminiscent of the French Empire. "It would be a sacrilege merely to 're-decorate' it—a word I hate," Jackie Kennedy told *Life* magazine. "It must be restored, and that has nothing to do with decoration."

Jackie Kennedy proudly took the nation on a tour of the newly restored White House on a live television broadcast on February 14, 1962. More than 80 million viewers tuned in. "The Kennedys made the White House a showcase of art, history and culture that influenced →

THE OLD FAMILY Dining Room was opened for public viewing in 2015 with a modern look. The room, which is used as an alternative to the State Dining Room, was outfitted with gray walls, red drapes and modern art. Featured on the north wall is "Resurrection"—a 1966 piece by Alma Thomas.

“

There are times when you run screaming, 'You can't put those hot television lights up against the portrait of Washington!'"

White House curator
William Allman

Trump hosted South Korean first lady Kim Jung-sook in the Green Room in April 2019.

the national identity," wrote Noel Grove in the book *Inside the White House.*

Today, the president and first lady make changes to the house to suit their own tastes, selecting pieces from the White House Collection. Items of particular historic importance tend to remain in place through changing administrations. For example, the Lincoln bed has remained in the White House nearly without interruption since it was first purchased by first lady Mary Todd Lincoln in 1861. The bed was intended for use in the main guest bedroom, so President Lincoln himself likely didn't sleep in it—though his son, William, sadly died in it at age 11 in 1862 from typhoid fever. Made of rosewood, the bed is nearly 6 feet wide and 8 feet long. Intricate carvings cover the headboard and footboard. It was part of a set of furniture costing $800. Today, it is in the southeast guest suite of the White House, known as the Lincoln Bedroom.

Since 1880, every president (save Presidents Lyndon Johnson, Nixon and Ford) has conducted the business of the nation from the Resolute desk. The desk was carved from the timbers of the ship

the *H.M.S. Resolute* and was given as a gift to President Rutherford B. Hayes by Queen Victoria. It's ornately carved, and the top is covered in red leather. President Franklin D. Roosevelt added a front panel, carved with the presidential seal, so that his legs, crippled from polio, would not be visible.

Part of the efforts during the Kennedy restoration of the White House included establishing the position of the White House curator. The curator cares for and manages the fine art, furniture and decorative objects in the vast collection. The White House has had seven curators since its first in 1961, with the most recent curator, William Allman, serving three presidents before retiring in 2017. He was in charge of this living museum: the rare place where people live and work among historical and valuable art.

THE CHINA ROOM

IN 1917, FIRST lady Edith Wilson created the Presidential Collection Room, now the China Room, to hold and display the collection of White House tableware. Through the 19th century, china used by presidents was sold at auctions, and the funds raised were used to purchase more furnishings. But after the establishment of the China Room, the White House began to track down pieces from the sets used by each president. The pieces aren't just for decoration, though. There are currently 18 sets of presidential china that are large enough for a complete state service. The Obamas unveiled their set at a state dinner for Japanese Prime Minister Shinzo Abe in 2015—blue and gold and stamped with the presidential seal.

★

CHAPTER 6

SECRET ROOMS

⫸⟶

★   ★   ★

THERE ARE A NUMBER OF SPACES THAT BRING WHIMSY AND LEISURE INTO THE OTHERWISE SERIOUS BUILDING.

BOWLING LANES WERE added to the ground floor of the White House as a gift for President Harry Truman in 1947 but were moved out less than a decade later. President Richard Nixon *(opposite)* returned the pins to the grounds, installing a one-lane alley in the basement during his tenure in office. It's still used by staffers, members of the Secret Service and visitors—in May 2011 alone, more than 200 people were cleared to bowl a few frames.

WHEN IT COMES TO FOOD *in Washington, D.C., there's no such thing as a best-kept secret. That goes double for dessert: If there's a restaurant or shop turning out worthy sweets in the nation's capital, rest assured that the city's treat-seekers know all about it.*

There is, however, an exception to this rule—a chocolate shop that serves top-of-the-line desserts to the president, as well as some of his most distinguished visitors. It's in the White House basement. ⟶

PRESIDENT Gerald Ford did push-ups in his pajamas in the Executive Residence on March 13, 1975; today, there's a private "workout room" on the third floor.

FIRST LADY PAT NIXON, who loved gardening, tried her hand at flower arranging in the White House in 1970.

The chocolate shop supplements the White House's pastry kitchen, helping produce the thousands and thousands of sweets consumed by guests each year. Pastry chefs begin preparing for the holiday season in June, and the crowning masterpiece—a replica of the White House, made from gingerbread and chocolate—takes hours and hours of detailed work.

It's a perfect example of the type of space in the White House that has come to be known as a "secret room." It's not nearly as well known or prestigious as, say, the Oval Office or the Lincoln Bedroom, but it's part of what makes 1600 Pennsylvania Avenue the unique, remarkable property that it is.

The basement is also home to the carpenters' and engineers' shops, which keep the furniture and machinery of the White House in top condition. So enamored was first lady Mamie Eisenhower with the fine craftsmen of the White House, she enlisted them in helping furnish the Eisenhowers' Gettysburg home.

Also underground is the bowling alley, used by a number of White House employees ranging from staffers to members of the Secret Service. But no one has enjoyed the lane more than Richard Nixon, who had the alley installed while in office. An enthusiastic but less-than-stellar sportsman, Nixon once excitedly told Henry Kissinger that he had shot a 147 that day. "Your golf is improving, Mr. President," Kissinger told him. "I was bowling," a dejected Nixon replied.

Nixon may have been the bowling alley's chief devotee, but President Jimmy Carter was the White House Family Theater's. A former coat room converted in 1942, the theater has seating for 42 guests ⟶

66

[The pool] will be one of the greatest pleasures for me during my stay in the White House."

President Franklin D. Roosevelt

————

IN 1965, LYNDON Johnson invited Gemini 4 astronauts to the White House, where they frolicked in the pool with their children.

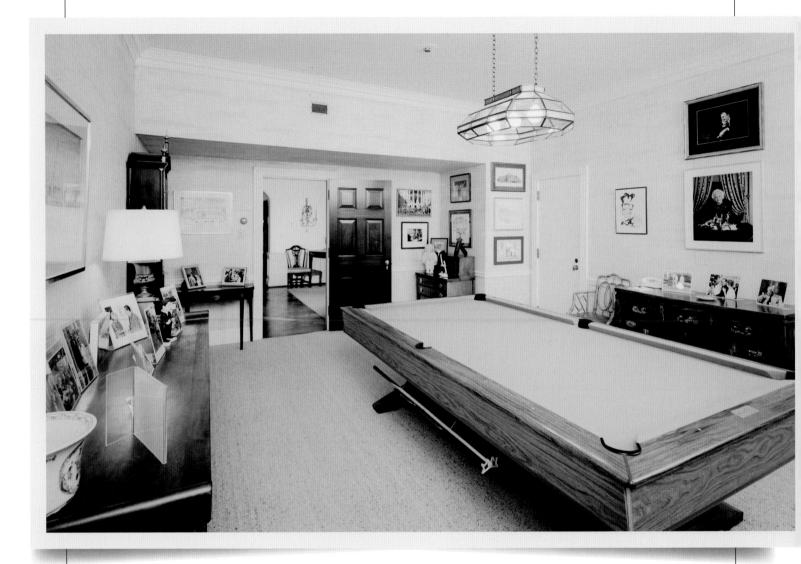

and screens everything from Hollywood classics to yet-to-be-released blockbusters. Carter was said to have taken in nearly 500 films during his time in office. His first? *All the President's Men,* just two days after he was sworn in as commander in chief.

There are opportunities at the White House for more refreshing forms of relaxation as well—namely, its swimming pool. Not wanting to displace the media from the Press Briefing Room that

THE COOLIDGE FAMILY spent a great deal of time in the Billiard Room in the 1920s, but that area has since been converted into the Map Room.

remains today over an indoor pool built for polio-stricken President Franklin Delano Roosevelt, President Gerald Ford arranged for an outdoor pool to be built in 1975. He and his wife Betty made a contribution of $500 of their own money to the project, labeling it as "our appreciation for what is being done to make this available for the White House and future presidents."

Plenty more rooms exist to allow for the behind-the-scenes work that makes

the White House function as smoothly as it does. On the second floor of the East Wing, the calligraphy office sees a team of highly skilled calligraphers hand-address up to 10,000 envelopes each holiday season. Since the Nixon administration, the cosmetology room in the Executive Residence has served as a beauty parlor. And first families aren't shy to change spaces for their own personalized needs: Hillary Clinton famously converted an

PRESIDENT CLINTON practiced the saxophone in a room that first lady Hillary turned into a makeshift rehearsal space as her birthday gift to him. The room had previously served as a bedroom for Gerald Ford's son Jack and a preschool room for John Kennedy Jr.

unused third-floor room into a rehearsal studio for President Bill Clinton and his beloved saxophone.

The White House is more than just a ceremonial center of power, steeped in history. It's a place to live as well, albeit a highly unusual one. The spaces off the beaten path, and away from the pomp and circumstance of the executive branch, are those that make the White House a home.

AMY CARTER CELEBRATED HER 10TH birthday on October 19, 1977, with a pumpkin-carving contest in the China Room. Woodrow Wilson's wife, Edith, began using the room for china in 1917, and every past president is represented by their official china or glassware.

PRESIDENT OBAMA RECEIVED AN H1N1 vaccine from a White House nurse on December 20, 2009. The White House medical unit on the ground floor, which includes a mini urgent care center and exam rooms near the Oval Office, serves staffers who work around the clock and may not have time to visit their own doctors.

WHEN HE WAS STILL CIA director, in 1976, George H. W. Bush got a haircut in the White House barbershop on the ground floor of the West Wing from longtime White House barber Milton Pitts. Reagan's Chief of Staff James Baker ended the privilege for anyone but the president and vice president in 1982, which caused "deep, but discreetly expressed, dismay," according to *The New York Times*.

PRESIDENT JIMMY CARTER sitting in front of the fireplace in the White House's ground-floor library on February 2, 1977. Furnished in the style of the late Federal period, it was remodeled from a former laundry area in 1935 and houses a wide collection of presidential papers.

OTHER PRESIDENTIAL RETREATS

CAMP DAVID, a huddle of secluded lodges and cabins in Maryland's Catoctin Mountain Park, is the country retreat for the president. The space was formally established in 1942 by President Franklin Delano Roosevelt, who wanted a place to get away from the heat and politics of Washington. Originally called Shangri-La, the getaway was renamed Camp David by President Dwight Eisenhower *(above right, with President Kennedy)*. Historic events, including the negotiation of the Camp David Accords in 1978 between Israel and Egypt, have occurred on its grounds.

Apart from Camp David, some presidents have maintained their own private residences as de facto retreats. President Richard Nixon's "Winter White House" was a home in Key Biscayne, Florida; he escaped there during the Watergate scandal. President George W. Bush spent time both at his family's summer compound in Kennebunkport, Maine, and Prairie Chapel Ranch in Texas during his presidency, and entertained foreign dignitaries at both locations. President Donald Trump's getaway is a private club he owns in Palm Beach, Florida, known as Mar-a-Lago.

THE WHITE HOUSE FAMILY THEATER WAS built in 1942 in the East Wing and adapted film screenings to presidents' tastes. Here, first lady Mamie Eisenhower is joined by her grandchildren, perhaps before a screening of one of Dwight D. Eisenhower's favorite Westerns; while in office, he watched over 200!

FIRST LADY BARBARA BUSH, WITH grandson "Jebby" Bush Jr., President George H. W. Bush and others, gathered in 1989 for a screening in the theater, which holds about 40 seats; the front row also included footstools for the presidents and their families. Their son, President George W. Bush, later used the room to practice his State of the Union addresses.

IN 2009, FIRST LADY Michelle and President Barack Obama (and others) tried out 3D glasses while watching the Super Bowl. (President George W. Bush had the theater redone in red in 2005.)

THE THEATER IS ALSO FOR GATHERINGS: On January 31, 1993, President Bill Clinton watched the Super Bowl with (*from left*) Texas Gov. Ann Richards; his daughter, Chelsea; New York Gov. Mario Cuomo; and Cuomo's wife, Matilda.

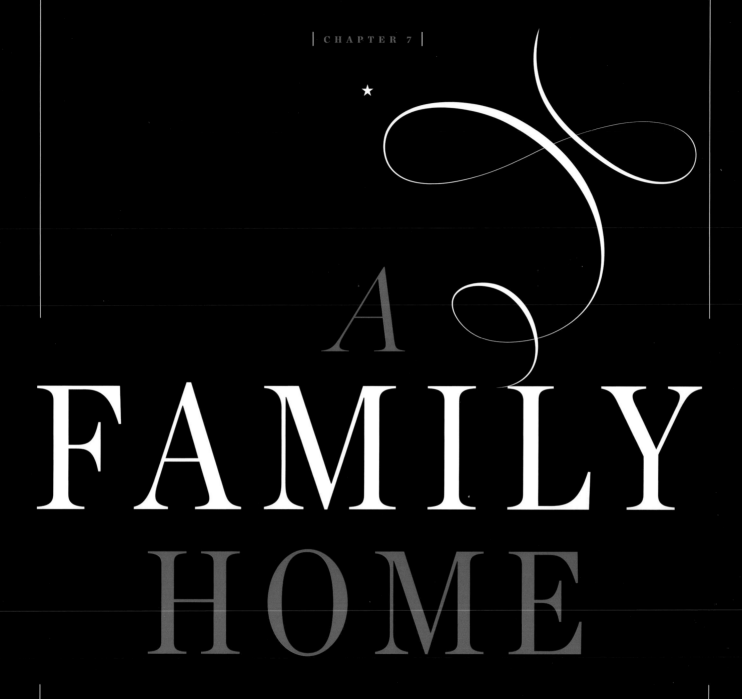

CHAPTER 7

A
FAMILY
HOME

★ ★ ★

THE WHITE HOUSE ISN'T JUST AN OFFICE BUILDING— IT'S WHERE CHILDREN GROW UP AND FAMILY EVENTS TAKE PLACE.

THE FIRST FAMILY—Hillary, Chelsea and Bill Clinton—walk their dog, Buddy, on the South Lawn of the White House in 1998. Chelsea was 12 when she moved into the White House, and she would go on to celebrate many milestones there, such as her Sweet 16. "It's the request of the president and Mrs. Clinton that Chelsea be allowed to have as normal a childhood as possible while living at the White House," said Neel Lattimore, the first lady's spokesman.

IN ONE OF the most famous photographs of President John F. Kennedy's time in office, he's sitting behind the Resolute desk, going through the papers of the day—and his son, 2-year-old John F. Kennedy Jr., is peeping out from below through the open panel of the desk. The images of the young president with his toddler children helped create the Camelot myth. The Kennedys were an ideal American family—polished, well-spoken—and the kids were adorable. →

LYNDON and Lady Bird Johnson welcomed the Nixons (Richard; Pat, in pink; and Tricia, in blue) to their future home on Nixon's Inauguration Day, January 20, 1969.

AT AGE 43, JOHN F. Kennedy became the youngest man to be elected president, and he brought with him a young family, including John Jr. (peeking out from the desk), who wasn't even 2 when he moved into the White House.

GEORGE W. BUSH'S
daughters, Jenna (*left*) and
Barbara, found it difficult
to escape the prying eyes
of the media and public
during their teen years.

Children in the White House bring a spark of fun and whimsy to the stately building. Quentin Roosevelt, son of Teddy and Edith, would lead a group of young boys around the building, play baseball on the lawn and shoot spitballs at historic paintings. Abraham and Mary's son Tad sold his parents' clothing in yard sales on the lawn, and Amy Carter, Jimmy and Rosalynn's daughter, roller-skated through the East Room.

But particularly in the modern era, with elevated security concerns and 24/7 news coverage, the White House isn't an easy place to grow up. "The staff knows everything you do," said Steve Ford, son of Gerald and Betty. Steve played Led Zeppelin from a stereo on the White House roof on the day they moved in, and it didn't go unnoticed: "Eugene, the butler, knew what we did, and I was so thankful that he never ratted me out to my parents."

Throughout the various presidencies, more than 20 children and adolescents have called the White House home, growing up and going to school under the watchful eye of the residence staff and the Secret Service, and under the constant →

AMY CARTER CELEBRATED her 11th birthday in the White House and got some help blowing out the candles from her mother, Rosalynn, and nephew James Earl Carter IV.

" Have fun and enjoy your childhood in such a magical place to live and play."

Barbara and Jenna Bush in a letter to Malia and Sasha Obama, 2009

———

surveillance of the public eye. Over the past few decades, a handful of kids—Malia and Sasha Obama, Chelsea Clinton, and twins Jenna and Barbara Bush, for example—spent eight years growing up in front of the American public.

Chelsea Clinton was 12 when her father was inaugurated in 1993. Despite her mother's attempt to limit media coverage, Chelsea was occasionally subject to petty or mean-spirited comments—some of which led former first daughter Margaret Truman to spring to her defense. "My sympathy is with Chelsea, since I, too, was hauled off to Washington—at the age of 11, when my father was elected to the Senate, and incarcerated in the White House when he became President," she wrote in *The New York Times.*

Jenna and Barbara Bush moved in next and brought more of a wild streak to the first family. They got their first taste of the White House when they would visit their grandfather, President George H. W. Bush. At age 7, they were sliding down banisters and bowling in the alley downstairs. They returned just before entering college, when their father, George W. Bush, was sworn in as president, and got into the same sorts of trouble other teenagers might. However, unlike other children, their transgressions would make the news.

IN APRIL 1933, first lady Eleanor Roosevelt played with her grandchildren on the White House lawn.

The Bush twins took their responsibility toward the next pair of first daughters seriously and wrote a letter to incoming first daughters Malia and Sasha Obama as they traded places. They advised them to keep their loyal friends close—as well as their animal friends —and slide down the banisters. And, most importantly, they wrote, "remember who your dad really is."

Malia and Sasha were 9 and 6 years old on Inauguration Day in January 2009. Like Chelsea Clinton, they attended Sidwell Friends School and brought friends around for sleepovers in the solarium. Their parents worked to keep their private lives private and to provide as normal an upbringing as possible.

Growing up in such a public space, under constant security and the watchful eye of staff, is challenging—but it does come with some perks. Malia Obama hosted her 18th birthday party on the grounds of the White House, and singers Kendrick Lamar and Janelle Monáe sang her "Happy Birthday." The presidents' children can also attend star-studded events, meet foreign dignitaries and travel the world. They have their own ceremonial duties as well, like participating in the annual Easter Egg Roll, Turkey Pardon and Christmas Tree Lighting ceremony.

Another perk? The White House has served as a wedding venue for nine children of presidents. In 1820, in the first of these ceremonies, Maria Hester Monroe, daughter of President James Monroe, married Samuel Lawrence Gouverneur in the Blue Room. Lynda Johnson, daughter of Lyndon and Lady Bird, was married in the East Room in 1967. And Tricia Nixon, daughter of Richard Nixon, had an outdoor wedding with almost 400 guests in the scenic Rose Garden.

THE OBAMA FAMILY gathered to watch the U.S. take on Japan in a World Cup soccer game in 2011.

PROUD GRANDPA GEORGE
H. W. Bush strolled with granddaughters Lauren (*left*) and Jenna in 1989.

GERALD FORD JOKINGLY
played peekaboo with daughter Susan in 1974.

PRESIDENT RONALD Reagan and grandson Cameron built a snowman in 1985.

PRESIDENT WOODROW WILSON *(fourth from left)* and his wife, Edith, celebrated daughter Jessie's wedding at the White House in 1913.

FIRST DAUGHTER TRICIA Nixon took her vows in the Rose Garden when she wed Edward Cox on June 12, 1971.

PROUD PAPA PRESIDENT
Lyndon Johnson looked on as daughter Luci cut her wedding cake on August 6, 1966, in the East Room.

PRESIDENT THEODORE
Roosevelt posed with his daughter Alice and his new son-in-law Nicholas Longworth on their wedding day in 1906, held in the renovated East Room.

★

LIFE
as a
FIRST PET

⫸⟶

★ ★ ★

FROM EXOTIC ANIMALS TO CATS AND CANINES, MANY FOUR-LEGGED AND FEATHERED FRIENDS HAVE MADE 1600 PENNSYLVANIA AVENUE HOME.

THE PETS Him and Her
THE PRESIDENT Lyndon B. Johnson (1963–1969)
LBJ's prized beagles lived the luxe life at 1600 Pennsylvania Avenue, from lounging in the Oval Office to swimming in the White House pool and romping through a specially designed doghouse, dubbed "a palace" by the press corps. Him and Her's superpup status was secured in 1964 when the endearing siblings made the cover of *Life* magazine. Unfortunately, a photograph in the publication featured Johnson lifting Him by his ears, sparking outrage from hundreds of angry dog lovers—much to LBJ's confusion.

THE PET **Macar**

THE PRESIDENT **John F. Kennedy (1961–1963)**
President Kennedy indulged his children, Caroline and John Jr., with practically a zoo's worth of pets. But when Caroline was given a part-Shetland pony named Macaroni by Lyndon Johnson, the cuteness factor went through the roof. The horse freely roamed the White House grounds and received thousands of fan letters from across the country. It's been said that a photo of Caroline riding Macaroni inspired Neil Diamond to write his iconic song "Sweet Caroline."

DATING BACK TO George Washington's extensive menagerie—which included three staghounds, four black and tan coonhounds, a horse and even a pair of donkeys— American presidents have displayed an abiding passion for pets. The White House has been home to well over 200 animal companions, ranging from the warm and fuzzy to the totally bizarre. Beginning with Thomas Jefferson, who was gifted a pair of grizzly bear cubs in 1807, presidents have often been presented with exotic animals, some of which were kept in the executive mansion (although many promptly found a home in a zoo). But mostly, it's been dogs (and an occasional cat) who have become part of the first family.

THE PETS Socks and Buddy
THE PRESIDENT Bill Clinton (1993-2001)

Before becoming first cat, Socks charmed his way into the Arkansas governor's mansion by jumping into the arms of Hillary and Bill Clinton's young daughter, Chelsea, as she was leaving her piano lesson one night. The stray was promptly adopted and became something of a Clinton family mascot, featuring in books, comics and even an episode of the hit show *Murphy Brown*. Sadly Socks' status took a hit in 1997 when the Clintons brought home Buddy, a scene-stealing chocolate Lab. According to the first lady, Socks "despised Buddy from first sight, instantly and forever." Ultimately, Socks went to live with the president's secretary, Betty Currie, due to ongoing issues with his canine rival. The president quipped, "I did better with the Palestinians and the Israelis than I've done with Socks and Buddy."

THE PET **Fala**
THE PRESIDENT **Franklin Delano Roosevelt** (1933–1945)
The most famous of FDR's pets was his beloved Scottish terrier, Fala. The pup gained notoriety during Roosevelt's 1944 reelection campaign, when Republican opponents charged that the president had sent a taxpayer-funded destroyer to fetch the dog from the Aleutian Islands, where he supposedly had been left behind. "I don't resent attacks, and my family doesn't resent attacks, but Fala does [and] his Scotch soul was furious. He has not been the same dog since," FDR told an audience. A statue of Fala with his master resides in Washington's FDR memorial, the only presidential pet to be so honored.

THE PETS Barney and Miss Beazley
THE PRESIDENT George W. Bush (2001–2009)
When "W" became the second Bush to reach the White House, it quickly became apparent that he was cut from the same dog-loving cloth as his parents, President George H. W. and Barbara Bush. His pride and joy was Barney, a black Scottish terrier who was never far from his master's side (or arms!)—except when it came time to board the helicopter, when the exuberant pooch would often have to be chased. Eternally loyal, the Scotty was often seen guarding the South Lawn entrance of the White House "as if he were a Secret Service agent," Bush joked. When Barney was 4, he was given a little "sister"—10-week-old Miss Beazley, also a black Scotty. Barney succumbed to lymphoma in 2013 at the age of 12; Miss Beazley died of the same disease the following year. "Barney was by my side during our eight years in the White House. He never discussed politics and was always a faithful friend," recalled Bush.

THE PETS Bo and Sunny

THE PRESIDENT Barack Obama (2009–2017)

President Obama's daughters lobbied long and hard to get a pet—and finally family friend Sen. Ted Kennedy obliged. In 2009, he presented the Obamas a cuddly black-and-white Portuguese water dog that would melt their hearts. They named the 6-month-old puppy Bo after rocker Bo Diddley, a moniker that would evolve into "Bobama." Reportedly, the Obamas initially intended to adopt a rescue dog, but ultimately chose a Portuguese water dog since the breed is considered to be hypoallergenic (daughter Malia suffers from allergies). Apparently, the first family couldn't get enough of a good thing. In 2013, they brought home a playmate for Bo: his "sister," Sunny, an all-black Portie. This pair of privileged pooches still lives in the Washington, D.C., area.

THE PET Rex
THE PRESIDENT Ronald Reagan (1981–1989)
The Reagans' first White House pooch, Lucky, was a spirited Bouvier des Flandres puppy who grew so massive—and rowdy!—that he had to be exiled to their California ranch. In December 1985, they got the more docile Rex, an adorable Cavalier King Charles spaniel who could often be seen cradled in first lady Nancy's arms. Rex made his Washington debut when he helped flip the switch to the White House Christmas tree lights, and from there proceeded to brighten the rest of the Reagan years for dog lovers everywhere.

THE PET Millie
THE PRESIDENT George H. W. Bush (1989–1993)
Perhaps the most accomplished—and certainly the highest earner—of first pets was Millie, the English springer spaniel who stole the show at the Bush White House. When the first lady "ghostwrote" *Millie's Book: As Dictated to Barbara Bush*, Millie's dog's-eye account of life in the executive mansion zoomed to No. 1 on *The New York Times*' Best Sellers list and raked in over $1 million for Mrs. Bush's Foundation for Family Literacy charity. Millie's six puppies included Spot "Spotty" Fetcher and Ranger, both of whom stayed in the Bush family.

WARREN HARDING GOT AN ENTHUSIASTIC greeting from his dog Laddie Boy in 1923. Among Harding's other pets: Pete, a squirrel.

GERALD FORD took a break in the Oval Office to greet his golden retriever, Liberty.

FIRST LADY GRACE Coolidge was enamored with white collies, including the Coolidges' dog Rob Roy.

FIRST DAUGHTER Amy Carter with her dog, Grits, in 1977; she also had a Siamese cat.

PRESIDENT HARRY Truman's cocker spaniel Feller frolicked on the lawn.

PRESIDENTIAL PET GOAT WHISKERS pulled Benjamin Harrison's young family members around the White House grounds as Harrison's dog, Jack, relaxed nearby. The family also kept a pair of possums as pets.

123

★

CHAPTER 9

The
GROUNDS

⋙⟶

★   ★   ★

WHITE HOUSE HISTORY DOESN'T ONLY RESIDE INSIDE ITS HALLS— IT LIVES AND BREATHES ON ITS LAWN.

TULIPS AND FLOWERING trees bloom in the White House Rose Garden in 1963 *(opposite)*. The area has been a source of beauty at the White House for over 100 years. However, prior to its conversion at the turn of the 20th century, it was a stable yard, housing horses and coaches for official use. Formerly located just outside the windows of the State Dining Room, the stables were moved to allow dining guests a view that wouldn't compromise their appetites. The first iteration of the Rose Garden, a "colonial garden" installed by Edith Roosevelt, was established in 1902, and the last White House stable was removed in 1911.

IN OCTOBER 2016, first lady Michelle Obama reflected on one of the first projects she launched after her husband was inaugurated seven years earlier: the White House Kitchen Garden. "I had this crazy idea: What if we planted a garden on the South Lawn to start a conversation about where our food comes from and how it impacts our children's health?" she told a crowd assembled on the White House lawn. "I take pride in knowing that this garden will serve as a reminder of what we all started." →

MICHELLE Obama pulled carrots alongside D.C.-area students in October 2009. The first lady frequently welcomed community members to help her tend to the White House Kitchen Garden.

POSITIONED JUST SOUTH of the East Colonnade, the Jacqueline Kennedy Garden—named by Lady Bird Johnson in 1965—remains one of the White House's most beautiful fixtures.

129

By the time first lady Michelle Obama made that dedication, her original dream had been realized: The 2,800-square-foot garden was turning out 2,000 pounds of fresh food for the White House, with extra produce being sent to a local charity. It was also an anchor for her Let's Move! initiative, which worked to combat childhood obesity with education on nutrition and exercise.

Michelle Obama was far from the first to make transformations to the lawn. In installing the White House Kitchen Garden, she was continuing a long tradition of reshaping, repurposing and beautifying its grounds. Today, the outdoor space surrounding the White House is lush with trees and flowers, and also includes recreational areas, such as a putting green, pool and tennis court.

From the very beginning, the White House grounds were considered an essential part of its construction. When Pierre Charles L'Enfant drew up his plans for Washington, D.C., he included an enormous 82-acre "President's Park," which covered the swath of land that stretched from what is now H Street to Constitution Avenue. That ambition, however, was deemed too grandiose.

"The ground about the president's house [is] much too extensive," David Stuart, one of the commissioners charged with designing the new capital city, said of L'Enfant's design. "It may suit the genius of a despotic government to cultivate an immense and gloomy wilderness in the midst of a thriving city.... I cannot think it suitable in our situation."

Instead, like the rest of the White House in its early days, the lawn was an ongoing project. When Thomas Jefferson took office in 1801, becoming the second president to live in the White House after John Adams, the lawn was a construction site. Jefferson established →

> "
> **What's great about the job is that our trees, our plants, our shrubs, know nothing about politics."**
>
> *Longtime White House head gardener Irvin Williams*

PRESIDENT GERALD Ford was a good sport after losing a friendly match to his son, Steve, shown jumping over the net, on the White House tennis court. The first court was built in 1902 by President Theodore Roosevelt, who played regular afternoon games with a group of local men he referred to as his "tennis cabinet." Today, the White House tennis court sits on the southwest grounds.

FIRST LADY LADY BIRD
Johnson posed on the
White House lawn beneath
an American elm tree
in 1967. She and her
husband were staunch
environmentalists, and
over 200 laws pertaining
to the environment were
passed during the Lyndon
Johnson administration.

the 18-acre parameters for the lawn that remain today, but much of the substantive planting he ordered went largely for naught: The British army's destruction of the White House under James Madison in 1814 undid much of his work, leaving James Monroe and his administration to orchestrate a rebuild. Monroe hired Frenchman Charles Bizet, who had worked on his family's Montpelier, Virginia, home, as the White House gardener. His successor, President John Quincy Adams, employed John Ousley into the same role. Ousley remained in the position for three decades.

Upon his inauguration in 1829, President Andrew Jackson moved to the White House with a heavy heart. That election cycle was one of the most brutal in American history, and Jackson's political rivals had relentlessly attacked the character of his wife, Rachel, throughout the process. When she passed away in December 1828, Jackson concluded that the stress of the campaign had brought about her death.

"My mind is so disturbed…that I scarcely write," Jackson said in a letter to a confidant. "In short, my dear heart is nearly broke."

In tribute to Rachel, Jackson planted a magnolia tree on the south grounds of the White House. The tree became an iconic fixture of the lawn, even earning a place on the back of the $20 bill for most of the 20th century. (In 2017, the White House announced that the historic Jackson Magnolia was in poor condition and needed to be cut—but healthy offshoots were planted as replacements.)

In total, nearly three dozen of the trees on the grounds were planted by presidents and first ladies. Other noteworthy trees include an American elm, planted by John Quincy Adams in 1826 and kept alive through a graft onto

IN 2019, FIRST LADY Melania Trump ceremonially broke ground (with a gold shovel) on the new tennis pavilion on the White House lawn. According to the National Park Service, which oversees the White House grounds, the pavilion will be clad in limestone and have a copper roof when completed.

a new tree in the 1990s, and a dogwood tree, planted by Bill Clinton in honor of the victims of the federal office building bombing in Oklahoma City.

"With its wonderful spring flower and its deep, enduring roots, it embodies the lesson of the Psalms that the life of a good person is like a tree whose leaf does not wither," Clinton said of the tree.

PRESIDENT BARACK
Obama and Vice President Joe Biden practiced on the putting green in 2009. When golf course architect Robert Trent Jones, Jr. had been designing the second iteration of the area, President Bill Clinton requested that a bunker be installed. A Secret Service agent advised, "If you build a bunker, his shots will hit the White House, the alarms will go off and we've got a Code Red." t

PRESIDENT GERALD FORD loved going for daily swims like this one on a hot day in August 1975, in the outdoor pool, right outside the Oval Office (and the press often showed up).

THE POOL WAS installed that year on the South Lawn.

DESPITE ITS NAME, the White House Rose Garden features a wide variety of flowers, including tulips, shown here in full bloom in the spring of 2007.

THE ROSE GARDEN

THE WHITE HOUSE Rose Garden is today frequently used for ceremonial events and announcements from the president. First lady Edith Roosevelt, who was overseeing renovations to the White House, added the garden space in 1902. Ten years later, it was converted into a rose garden.

In 1962, horticulturist Rachel Lambert Mellon was charged with revamping the space, creating an open lawn cornered by magnolias and filled with flowers. "These trees would soften the difficult corners that were now bare and would permit sufficient light to fall beneath and around them to allow planting," she wrote.

Soon after it was completed, John F. Kennedy used the Rose Garden to swear in secretaries and entertain dignitaries. In the years that followed, the garden was used for a host of events—including the wedding of Tricia Nixon, President Richard Nixon's daughter, on June 12, 1971.

Among the types of roses planted there are the Queen Elizabeth, the Pat Nixon and the King's Ransom varieties.

PRESIDENT FRANKLIN D. Roosevelt's grandchildren enjoyed the playground in 1933.

FIRST DAUGHTER LUCI Johnson Nugent played with son Patrick in 1968.

FIRST DAUGHTER Amy Carter and pals romped in her tree house in 1978.

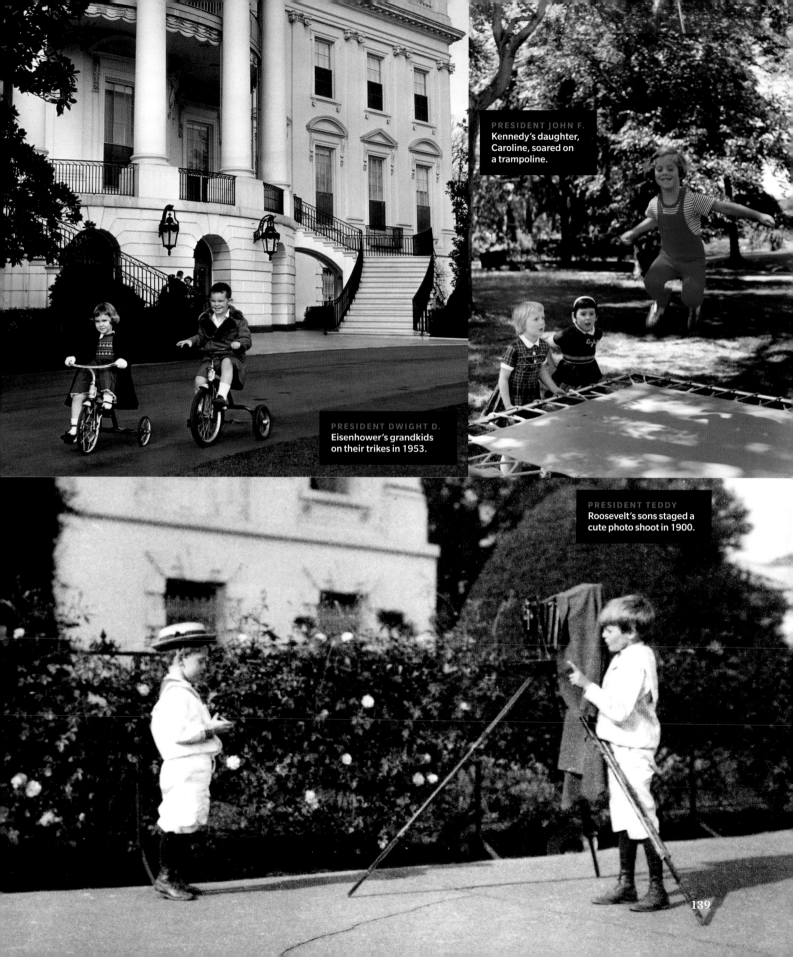

PRESIDENT JOHN F. Kennedy's daughter, Caroline, soared on a trampoline.

PRESIDENT DWIGHT D. Eisenhower's grandkids on their trikes in 1953.

PRESIDENT TEDDY Roosevelt's sons staged a cute photo shoot in 1900.

CHAPTER 10

HOLIDAYS *at the* WHITE HOUSE

★ ★ ★

WHEN IT COMES TO CELEBRATIONS—AND TRADITIONS PAST AND PRESENT—NO HOME SHINES BRIGHTER.

PRESIDENT GEORGE W. BUSH and first lady Laura Bush stand in front of the Blue Room's Christmas tree in December 2007. The first couple always made sure to deck the White House halls with extravagance during the holiday season. As for the Christmas holiday itself, the Bushes spent the day at the Camp David presidential retreat in Maryland. It was a habit George W. picked up from his father, former President George H. W. Bush.

"SANTA CLAUS IN WASHINGTON," *proclaimed the front page of* The New York Times *on December 25, 1889. The article painted the scene of a Christmas at President Benjamin Harrison's White House. That year, the first Christmas tree ever placed in the White House was in the Blue Bedroom: "Foxtail hemlock, 8 or 9 feet high, liberally decked with glittering glass balls and pendants...showered over with countless strands of gold tinsel," the Gray Lady gushed.* →

THE WHITE House Easter Egg Roll has been a favorite annual activity since the 1870s—and these kids in 1953 carried on the festive tradition.

THE OBAMA WHITE
House celebrated the day of July 4, 2010, with military pomp in conventional Executive Office style. (That night, though, featured something a little different: Rock band The Killers played a holiday White House concert.)

At the time, the White House Christmas was a small celebration, contained within the residence, for the first family and friends. But as the presidency entered the 20th century, Christmas—along with other major holidays—grew into gatherings for the nation. In 1903, for example, President Theodore Roosevelt opened the White House doors to nearly 500 children for a Christmas carnival. President Calvin Coolidge lit the first National Christmas Tree, a fir

PRESIDENT DWIGHT Eisenhower presided over the National Thanksgiving Presentation, a tradition started in 1947 as a way for the poultry and egg industries to promote their products. Turkeys these days are pardoned and sent to live on a Virginia farm.

from his home state of Vermont, in 1923. Each president since has continued the tradition. President George W. Bush hosted the first formal Hanukkah party at the White House in 2001 and lit the menorah for the second night of the eight-day holiday.

For the White House's pastry chefs, the marathon of the winter holiday season starts in June, with fruitcakes. "We gather all the ingredients—the nuts and the dried, candied and macerated fruits necessary to bake a half-ton of fruitcakes," wrote Roland Mesnier, former White House ⟶

147

executive pastry chef, in *The White House in Gingerbread: Memories & Recipes*. The chefs make gallons of ganache and mousse, piles of cakes—and the 25 to 30 sheets of gingerbread they need to construct their main holiday centerpiece: the White House gingerbread house.

Assistant executive chef Hans Raffert built the first White House gingerbread house for President Richard Nixon in 1969. The houses have grown more and more elaborate each year: In 1992, for

example, Mesnier built a to-scale replica of the White House itself. The pastry chefs set up shop in the China Room, "along with the tools needed to create the large-scale gingerbread house—a large band saw, measuring and cutting instruments, a commercial mixer, a personal pastry toolbox and several chocolate warmers," wrote Mesnier.

President Abraham Lincoln declared Thanksgiving Day a national holiday and was also the first president to

officially pardon a turkey—though it wasn't a Thanksgiving turkey. "A live turkey had been brought home for the Christmas dinner, but [Lincoln's son Tad] interceded in behalf of its life," wrote White House reporter Noah Brooks. President George H. W. Bush formally established the tradition of a Thanksgiving turkey pardon that continues to this day. In 2019, President Donald Trump spared two turkeys named Bread and Butter.

Fourth of July at the White House is always festive, with parades, fireworks and live music. President Thomas Jefferson opened the doors to the White House for a public reception to mark the holiday in 1801. President Barack Obama welcomed 5,000 guests to the South Lawn on that date in 2016. "The Fourth of July is about family," he said. "It's about the American family, it's about us getting together with the people we love most."

151

ROSALYNN CARTER—WITH daughter Amy and her costumed friends—got into the Halloween spirit in 1978.

THE OBAMAS CREATED these gourd "trees" for the North Portico of the White House in 2010.

PRESIDENT HARRY
Truman was visited by
friends (some of whom
didn't get into the
Thanksgiving spirit!).

THE WHITE HOUSE CHRISTMAS TREE

THOUGH CHRISTMAS trees were placed around the White House starting in the late 1890s, the tree did not become an annual official fixture until first lady Lou Henry Hoover started decorating a tree in 1929. When first lady Jackie Kennedy took charge of the White House Christmas tree—which stood in the Blue Room—in 1961, she decorated it in the theme of *The Nutcracker*, complete with toys and characters from the Tchaikovsky ballet.

Since then, themes have ranged from angels in 1993—which saw the tree covered with angel ornaments and decorations from over 1,000 artists—to first lady Barbara Bush's family literacy tree in 1989, adorned with 80 literary characters and mini books alongside them. Bush reprised the *Nutcracker* theme the following year, complete with a castle from the Land of Sweets.

In 2007, the theme was Holiday in the National Parks, with a handmade ornament for each park site. S. Christine Hall of Genoa, Wisconsin, an art teacher, painted the ornament for the Effigy Mounds National Monument in Iowa, and was invited to attend a holiday reception in honor of the theme at the White House. "The decorations were opulent and impressive," Hall said of the event. "The desserts were works of art that I felt guilty eating."

FIRST LADY PAT NIXON'S 1969 tree ornaments represented each state's flower; here, she decorated the tree with first daughter Julie (*left*).

PRESIDENT LYNDON AND Lady Bird Johnson's pup Yuki joined the fun in 1967. Their daughter Luci had found the dog at a gas station in 1966.

FIRST LADY MELANIA Trump opted for bold red trees for Christmas 2018.

PRESIDENT GEORGE H. W.
Bush had a rapt audience
when he read stories to his
grandchildren on Christmas
Eve at the White House in 1991.

159

★

CHAPTER 11

STATE
DINNERS

⇛⟶

★ ★ ★

THE SITE OF SOME OF HISTORY'S MOST GLAMOROUS PARTIES, THE WHITE HOUSE HAS HOSTED HUNDREDS OF WORLD LEADERS AND INTERNATIONAL CELEBRITIES.

FRANK SINATRA DANCED with first lady Nancy Reagan at the surprise 70th birthday party she threw for her husband, President Ronald Reagan, on February 6, 1981. A guest called the evening "an absolute smash hit."

THE FIRST STATE DINNER *in Washington, D.C., took place in December 1874, when King David Kalākaua—the last king of the Kingdom of Hawaii—paid a visit to Ulysses S. Grant's White House. First lady Julia Grant pulled out all the stops for him and his delegation, including a 587-piece set of antique French china. King Kalākaua greatly enjoyed his visit, which also featured a trip to New York City with his friend Mark Twain, and in January a treaty was signed to permit the tax-free import of goods into the U.S. from Hawaii.* ⟶

PRINCESS Diana shared a dance with John Travolta at a White House state dinner in 1985. "I'm so honored that I was able to experience it," the actor later said.

THE ROSE GARDEN was transformed into an elegant outdoor venue on a balmy late-spring night in 2011 when President Barack Obama and first lady Michelle Obama hosted a state dinner for German Chancellor Angela Merkel. About 200 guests attended the event, where Obama presented Merkel with the Medal of Freedom.

165

Thus began a long tradition of state dinners at the White House, in which visiting heads of state are feted by the American president and first lady. Over the years, state dinners took different shapes and forms based on what was happening in the country—or to the White House itself. During the two World Wars, state dinners were less extravagant in their decorations and feasts, so as not to project clueless opulence during hard times. And when the White House was undergoing renovations between 1948 and 1952, President Harry Truman hosted state dinners at D.C. hotels—although the Carlton hardly qualified as a downgrade.

In recent decades, presidents have taken to dazzling their international guests with performances by A-list musical talent. Bill Clinton impressed King Mohammed VI of Morocco with a set from Earth, Wind & Fire in 2000, and George W. Bush brought out country superstar Kenny Chesney to entertain Australian Prime Minister John Howard in 2006. Mexican President Felipe Calderón may have been the luckiest of all, as he and President Obama were treated to a Beyoncé concert at a 2010 state dinner.

But as effortless as it all seems in the moment, the pomp of a state dinner does not appear with the snap of a finger: Internal preparations for hosting such an event take at least six months. And leading the charge is typically the first lady, for whom the planning of a state dinner presents an opportunity to make her mark on the White House. As the third-youngest first lady in the history of the country, Jackie Kennedy was eager to do just that in organizing the first state dinner of the JFK administration, held in May 1961 for Tunisian President Habib Bourguiba. She dug into the White House archives to study past state dinners and draw inspiration from them, and she used her enthusiasm ⟶

66

This is not only a state dinner; it's like a family gathering."

President George W. Bush to Mexican President Vicente Fox

——

DURING A DINNER given in his honor by President John F. Kennedy, former President Harry Truman played an impromptu rendition of Paderewski's "Minuet in G" in the East Room. It was the first White House event held for Truman since he left office. Pianist Eugene List, standing, also played selections from Chopin at the 1961 event.

QUEEN ELIZABETH II and George W. Bush (*above*) raised a toast at a state dinner in May 7, 2007. The queen and Prince Philip attended the fete, which was the first white-tie event hosted by Bush and his wife, Laura, the first lady.

THIS OPULENT PLACE setting (*left*) was used for the state dinner Bush hosted in honor of Australian Prime Minister John Howard on May 16, 2006.

for the culinary arts to concoct a menu that would appeal to her foreign guests.

More than 50 years later, first lady Melania Trump was similarly motivated to put on a showstopping event for French President Emmanuel Macron in 2018. She chose a cream-and-gold color scheme, and devised a menu that included lamb and jambalaya. The first lady paid respects to her French guests by wearing a Chanel haute couture gown and serving wine grown from French vines in Oregon.

In planning these events, Kennedy and Trump—and every other first lady who has put on a state dinner—did so with a key ally: the White House Social Secretary. A position originated by Belle Hagner in 1901 during President Theodore Roosevelt's administration, the social secretary heads the Social Office in the East Wing. According to Hagner, the job chose her—not the other way around.

"I would like to say that ever since this position was created for me, I have always felt very strongly that the job of secretary to the president's wife is one which should not be solicited," said Hagner, who served a second stint in the role under President Woodrow Wilson. "I am happy to say that both times in my case, I was asked to take the place, without ever raising a finger to get it." ⟶

PRESIDENT GERALD
Ford shared a laugh
with Queen Elizabeth II at
a July 7, 1976, state dinner.
On the menu that night was
New England lobster and
saddle of veal, served
with an assortment of
American wines.

Perhaps the best-known social secretary was Letitia Baldrige, a longtime friend of Jackie Kennedy who came to the White House to serve in the position. Baldrige was an etiquette expert who appeared on the cover of *Time* magazine and on *Late Night With David Letterman*. In 2011, Jeremy Bernard became both the first male and the first openly gay social secretary for the Obamas. First lady Melania Trump's social secretary is Anna Cristina Niceta Lloyd, who boasts decades of experience in planning presidential inaugurations and various State Department events.

FRENCH PRESIDENT
Emmanuel Macron was the guest of honor during the first state dinner hosted by President Donald Trump, in April 2018. First lady Melania Trump planned the menu, which included a goat cheese gateau, spring rack of lamb and crème fraîche ice cream.

The State Dining Room has seating for up to 120 people, who are seated at assorted round tables. Hosts actively strive to create interesting, diverse seating arrangements and guests find their seats by handwritten place cards from the White House Graphics and Calligraphy office. Like just about everything else in the White House, a state dinner is an exceedingly formal event—but that doesn't mean it's stuffy.

Said former White House chef Walter Scheib, "A state dinner is so much more like a Broadway play than a dinner."

NELSON MANDELA'S VISIT

WHILE EVERY STATE dinner at the White House is a special affair, some take on increased significance due to circumstance. Such was certainly the case when South African President Nelson Mandela visited the Clinton White House on October 4, 1994.

After spending 27 years in prison for his opposition to apartheid in South Africa, Mandela was released in 1990 and, remarkably, elected president in May 1994. Months later,

he was greeted with a lavish state dinner at the White House.

The exceptionally large event was hosted in the East Room—where President Lyndon Johnson had signed the Civil Rights Act of 1964—and its near-200 guests included American civil rights icons including Jesse Jackson and Maya Angelou.

Speaking directly to Mandela, President Clinton said, "I ask all my fellow Americans to raise their glasses to you and all who have led South Africa into the bright light of freedom."

ACTRESS AND DANCER
Ann-Margret entertained the Shah of Iran at a state dinner hosted by Gerald and Betty Ford on May 15, 1975.

COMEDIAN MARTY ALLEN
and first lady Betty Ford cut a rug at a September 21, 1976, state dinner for the president of Liberia.

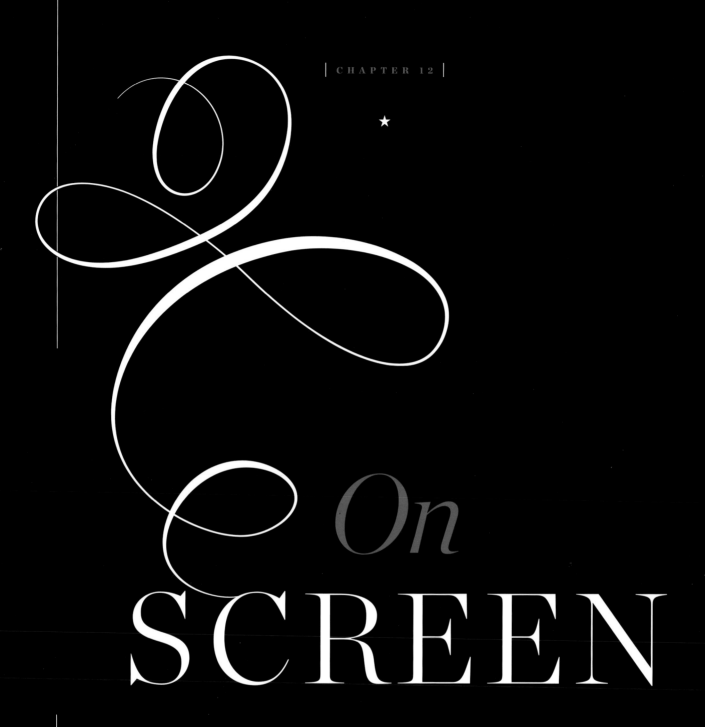

CHAPTER 12

& On SCREEN

★ ★ ★

FROM BIG-BUDGET BLOCKBUSTERS TO AWARD-WINNING SERIES, THE WHITE HOUSE HAS ALWAYS BEEN READY FOR ITS CLOSE-UP.

▶ *INDEPENDENCE DAY* (FILM; 1996) This blockbuster about an alien invasion, starring Bill Pullman as the president, brought the White House to life—including scenes in the master bedroom, private dining room, Oval Office and more—before blowing the building to smithereens. According to Pete Sharkey, writing for the White House Museum website, the scenes inside the building are filled with "accurate artwork and furnishings," but the press briefing room is "much too big." Still, the film, also starring Will Smith, Randy Quaid and Jeff Goldblum, packed enough box-office power to become one of the most successful films of the '90s.

▲ **THE WEST WING (SERIES; 1999–2006)**
Set in the titular area of the White House where senior staff work, Aaron Sorkin's award-winning behind-the-scenes drama of life in the administration of President Josiah Bartlet (Martin Sheen) gave audiences an inside look at working in the White House. With its famed rapid-fire dialogue, the show won 17 Emmys over its seven-year run.

WHENEVER IT'S ON SCREEN, the nation's most iconic seat of power and government is depicted in all its glory and complexity. Screenwriter Aaron Sorkin, who brought us the hit series The West Wing *from 1999 to 2006, says the White House is a place he couldn't resist featuring. While researching the 1995 romantic comedy* The American President, *which he also wrote, Sorkin noted, "I looked at presidential diaries going back to [Lyndon] Johnson and saw that the White House as a workplace was reinvented with every administration." These films and TV shows reflect how the "people's house" can be a star in its own right.* ⟶

▲ *VEEP* (SERIES; 2012–2019)

HBO's political satire starring Julia Louis-Dreyfus as twice-elected Selina Meyer took viewers into the halls of 1600 Pennsylvania Avenue and was praised by President Obama's former aides as an accurate representation of life inside the White House. But where it really excelled was in managing to "nail the fragility of the egos, and the, like, day-to-day idiocy of the decision-making," said podcaster Tommy Vietor.

◄ *HOUSE OF CARDS* (SERIES; 2013–2018)

The Netflix series starred Kevin Spacey as the conniving Frank Underwood, who schemed his way into the Oval Office only to have his equally diabolical wife, Claire, played by Robin Wright, outmaneuver him. The production designer for the show's first four seasons, Steve Arnold, told *Architectural Digest* he went through records and photos from the Historical American Buildings Survey to nail down the accuracy, but took some liberties. "You try to get as much of the character's story as possible into the set," he said.

◀ *LEE DANIELS' THE BUTLER* (FILM; 2013)

In this behind-the-scenes look at the White House, loosely based on fact, Forest Whitaker starred as Cecil Gaines, who served eight presidents over 34 years and bore witness to how the house itself can change as administrations arrive and others move on. "Cecil becomes an activist in his own small way, too, asking for equal pay for the black White House staff, and he finally wins out on that one," says Whitaker. "Small victories, big victories, they're all victories."

▲ *DESIGNATED SURVIVOR* (SERIES; 2016–2019)

With Kiefer Sutherland playing a Cabinet member thrust into the presidency after a brutal attack that kills everyone before him in the line of succession, the series presented a White House that drew from FDR (the draperies), Nixon (the flags) and Obama (the striped wallpaper) to replicate the Oval Office. Although it's a set, Sutherland said acting in the replica had a profound effect on him: "I will go on a set like the Oval Office and find myself sitting straighter there," he told *Parade* in 2017. "You feel a really heavy weight when you walk into that room. And I know it's fake."

▼ *WILSON* (FILM; 1944)

Starring Alexander Knox as President Woodrow Wilson, this film won five Oscars, including for Best Art Direction-Color. "The private quarters were carefully researched and painstakingly built from exact measurements and photographs," notes the White House Museum website. And while it may present a too-sunny dramatization of Wilson's tenure, the house itself is "beautifully recreated."

▶ *JACKIE* (FILM; 2016)
Natalie Portman earned an Oscar nomination for her turn as Jacqueline Kennedy in this film about the first lady following John F. Kennedy's assassination. Production designer Jean Rabasse focused on the little details of Jackie's White House bedroom, including fabrics from Tillett Textiles, to portray the White House accurately. "We tried to cheat as little as possible," he told *Architectural Digest*. "You can't imagine how far we went in the details, even in the moldings and paintings. We had copies or scans of every painting."

◀ *THE AMERICAN PRESIDENT* (FILM; 1995)
Michael Douglas is President Andrew Shepherd, a widower who falls for lobbyist Sydney Ellen Wade (Annette Bening) despite their being on opposite sides of a crime-bill debate. Director Rob Reiner visited the White House five times to prep for the movie, following around then-President Bill Clinton and gathering details about the house. The Oval Office set used in the film also appears in 1995's *Nixon* and 1996's *Independence Day*.

The White House
QUIZ

TEST YOUR KNOWLEDGE OF 1600 PENNSYLVANIA
AVENUE AND THE LIVES OF ITS OCCUPANTS.

1.

WHO DESIGNED
THE WHITE HOUSE?

A. FREDERICK LAW OLMSTED

B. PIERRE CHARLES L'ENFANT

C. JAMES HOBAN

D. DR. WILLIAM THORNTON

2. Who was the first president to live in the White House?

A. George Washington

B. John Adams

C. Thomas Jefferson

D. James Madison

3. Who created the White House Library?

A. President Millard Fillmore

B. President Thomas Jefferson

C. President Bill Clinton

D. President Calvin Coolidge

4. Where are the offices of the first lady?

A. Capitol Hill

B. The Eisenhower Executive Office Building

C. The East Wing

D. The West Wing

5. Which president has been portrayed in more movies than any other?

A. George Washington

B. Abraham Lincoln

C. Thomas Jefferson

D. Theodore Roosevelt

6. Thanks to a gift from the Sultan of Oman, Martin Van Buren was temporarily the owner of two of what animal—before Congress made him donate them to the zoo?

A. Tiger cubs

B. Turtles

C. Camels

D. Vultures

7. WHAT IS THE NICKNAME OF THE PRESIDENTIAL LIMO?

A. THE TANK

B. THE EAGLE

C. AIR FORCE THREE

D. THE BEAST

8. Which of the following rooms have never been a part of the White House?

A. Bowling alley

B. Chocolate shop

C. Darkroom

D. Music studio

9. What is the name of the famous presidential desk, built from the timbers of a ship?

A. The Titanic desk

B. The Resolute desk

C. The Victory desk

D. The Constitution desk

10. Which president watched the most movies (480) in the White House Family Theater?

A. President Ronald Reagan

B. President Richard Nixon

C. President Jimmy Carter

D. President George W. Bush

Answers: 1. C, 2. B, 3. A, 4. C, 5. B, 6. A, 7. D, 8. C, 9. B, 10. C

The White House
BY THE NUMBERS

THE FACTS AND FIGURES THAT DESCRIBE
AMERICA'S MOST FAMOUS HOME

55,000

SQUARE FEET ON 18 ACRES OF LAND

*The White House property sits in a 77-acre area known as
President's Park, which also includes Lafayette Square,
The Ellipse and the White House Visitor Center.*

412	3	28	147	8	35
DOORS	ELEVATORS	FIREPLACES	WINDOWS	STAIRCASES	BATHROOMS

...plus a bowling alley, movie theater, tennis court, putting green and more.

96
FULL-TIME
RESIDENCE
STAFFERS

250
PART-TIME
RESIDENCE
STAFFERS

5
FULL-TIME
CHEFS

*White House staff is under the direction
of the chief usher, a position currently
held by Timothy Harleth.*

65,000
TOTAL OBJECTS IN
THE ART COLLECTION

500
PAINTINGS IN
THE ART COLLECTION

*The first-ever piece acquired by the White House
art collection was Gilbert Stuart's 1796
portrait of George Washington.*

$232,372
ORIGINAL COST

$90M–$349M
RANGE OF ESTIMATES
FOR VALUE TODAY

*The historical value of the White House makes it
impossible to put a price on, but that doesn't
mean appraisal enthusiasts haven't tried. A 2016
estimate by real estate website Zillow estimated the
building to have a value of nearly $350 million.*

5,000
DAILY VISITORS

*Requests for tours must be made at least
21 days in advance, so be sure to plan ahead.*

570
GALLONS OF PAINT NEEDED
TO COVER EXTERIOR

*The paint color, made by Duron, is
known as Whisper White.*

COVER Narvikk/Getty **FRONT FLAP** Muni Yogeshwaran/Getty 1 Duncan1890/Getty **2-3** Eurobanks/Shutterstock **4-5** Clockwise from top left: Thomas D Mcavoy/The LIFE Picture Collection/Getty; Smith Collection/Gado/Getty; Bettmann/Getty; Dirck Halstead/The LIFE Images Collection/Getty **6-7** Brooks Kraft/Corbis/Getty **10-11** Library of Congress **12-13** Fine Art Images/ Heritage Images/Getty **14-15** Illustration by Cyprian Lothringer **18-19** Brendan Smialowski/AFP/Getty **20-21** From left: Glasshouse Images/ Shutterstock; Corbis/Getty **22-23** Bettmann/Getty **24-25** From left: Bettmann/Getty; Pete Souza/The White House/Getty **26-27** From left: Joe Raedle/Getty; Antonio Bolfo/Getty **28-29** Charles Ommanney/Getty **32-33** Smith Collection/ Gado/Getty **34-35** From left: PhotoQuest/Getty; Smith Collection/Gado/Getty **36-37** From left: Print Collector/Getty; Archive Photos/Getty; George Rinhart/Corbis/Getty **38-39** From left: Thomas D Mcavoy/The LIFE Picture Collection/Getty; Francis Miller/The LIFE Picture Collection/Getty **40-41** Smith Collection/Gado/Getty **42-43** From left: Ed Clark/The LIFE Picture Collection/Getty; Bettmann/Getty **44-45** Clockwise from top left: Lyndon B. Johnson Presidential Library and Museum/NARA; Brendan Smialowski/AFP/Getty; Archistoric/Alamy; Hum Images/Alamy **48-49** John F. Kennedy Library/Getty **50-51** From left: The White House/Handout/Getty; Abbie Rowe/PhotoQuest/Getty **52-53** Ronald Reagan Presidential Library and Museum/ NARA **54-55** From left: Horst P. Horst/Conde Nast/ Getty; Bettmann/Getty **56-57** From left: Everett Collection/Shutterstock; National Archives and Records Administration **58-59** Clockwise from top left: Jimmy Carter Presidential Library and Museum/ NARA; Carol T. Powers/White House/CNP/DPA Alliance/Alamy; Brooks Kraft LLC/Corbis/Getty; Bettmann/Getty **60-61** From left: Courtesy of Henry & Carole Haller and Family; Shutterstock **62-63** Clockwise from top left: Heikki Saukkoma/Shutterstock; Caroline Brehman/CQ-Roll Call, Inc/Getty; Brooks Kraft LLC/Corbis/Getty; Gabriel Piper/US Navy/Getty; Susan Walsh/AP **66-67** The LIFE Picture Collection/Getty **68-69** From left: VCG Wilson/Corbis/Getty; Natrot/Shutterstock; Horst P. Horst/ Conde Nast/Getty **70-71** Bill O'Leary/The The Washington Post/Getty **72-73** White House Photo/Alamy **74-75** From left: White House Photo/Planetpix/Alamy; Alex Wong/Getty **78-79** Bettmann/Getty **80-81** Clockwise from top left: Yale Joel/The LIFE Picture Collection/Getty (2); Jack E. Kightlinger/Wikimedia Commons; David Hume Kennerly/Getty **82-83** © 1965 White House Historical Association **84-85** From left: Library of Congress; Bob McNeely and White House Photograph Office/Clinton Digital Library **86-87** Clockwise from top left: Jimmy Carter Presidential Library and Museum/ NARA; David Hume Kennerly/Getty; Pete Souza/White House/Getty **88-89** From left: Corbis/Getty; National Archive/Newsmakers/Getty **90-91** Clockwise from top left: Ed Clark/The LIFE Picture Collection/Getty; Pete Souza/American Photo Archive/Alamy; Mark Reinstein/Alamy; George Bush Presidential Library and Museum/NARA **94-95** Smith Collection/Gado/Getty **96-97** Bettmann/Getty (2) **98-99** From left: Brendan Smialowski/AFP Photo/Getty; Bettmann/Getty **100-101** Bettmann/Getty **102-103** Pete Souza/The White House/Getty **104-105** Clockwise from top left: Bettmann/Getty; Ira Schwarz/AP/Shutterstock; David Hume Kennerly/Getty **106-107** Alex Wong/Getty **108-109** Clockwise from top left: E. D. Edmonston/Library of Congress; G. James/ Zuma; Print Collector/Getty; Bettmann/Getty **112-113** From left: Francis Miller/The LIFE Picture Collection/Getty; Bettmann/Getty **114-115** From left: Robert Knudsen/White House/Gamma-Rapho/Getty; Smith Collection/Gado/Getty **116-117** From left: Science History Images/ Alamy; Mandel Ngan/AFP/Getty **118-119** From left: White House Photo/ Alamy; Pete Souza/Pictorial Parade/Archive Photos/ Getty **120-121** David Valdez/White House via CNP/Getty **122-123** Clockwise from top left: Library of Congress/Getty; Everett Collection Inc/Alamy; Thomas D. Mcavoy/The LIFE Picture Collection/Getty; Glasshouse Vintage/Universal History Archive/ Getty; Hum Historical/Alamy; Bettmann/Getty **126-127** George Silk/The LIFE Picture Collection/Getty **128-129** From left: Tim Sloan/AFP Photo/Getty; Horst P. Horst/Conde Nast/Getty **130-131** David Hume Kennerly/White House/The LIFE Images Collection/Getty **132-133** From left: Horst P. Horst/Condé Nast/Getty; Andrea Hanks/White House/Zuma **134-135** Pete Souza/ White House/Getty **136-137** Clockwise from top left: David Hume Kennerly/Getty; Mannie Garcia/AFP Photo/Getty; Gerald R. Ford Presidential Library and Museum/NARA **138-139** Clockwise from top left: PhotoQuest/Getty; Everett Collection/ Shutterstock; John F. Kennedy Presidential Library and Museum/NARA; Everett Collection/Shutterstock; Frank Wolfe/White

CENTENNIAL BOOKS

An Imprint of
Centennial Media, LLC
40 Worth St., 10th Floor
New York, NY 10013, U.S.A.

CENTENNIAL BOOKS is a trademark of Centennial Media, LLC

ISBN 978-1-951274-41-2
Distributed by
Simon & Schuster, Inc.
1230 Avenue of the Americas
New York, NY 10020, U.S.A.

For information about custom editions, special sales and premium and corporate purchases,
please contact Centennial Media at contact@centennialmedia.com.

Manufactured in Malaysia

© 2020 by Centennial Media, LLC

10 9 8 7 6 5 4 3 2 1

Publishers & Co-Founders Ben Harris, Sebastian Raatz
Editorial Director Annabel Vered
Creative Director Jessica Power
Executive Editor Janet Giovanelli
Deputy Editors Ron Kelly, Alyssa Shaffer
Design Director Ben Margherita
Art Directors Andrea Lukeman,
Natali Suasnavas, Joseph Ulatowski
Assistant Art Director Jaclyn Loney
Photo Editor Keri Pruett
Production Manager Paul Rodina
Production Assistant Alyssa Swiderski
Editorial Assistant Tiana Schippa
Sales & Marketing Jeremy Nurnberg